ideals®

Durkee
Spice and Herb
Cookbook

D1410949

Ideals Publishing Corp.
Nashville, Tennessee

Contents

Cover recipes:
 Honey Spiced Ham, page 27
 Herbed Bubble Bread, page 47
 Mulled Cranberry Syllubub, page 13

ISBN 0-8249-3020-7

Copyright © MCMLXXXIII by Durkee Famous Foods,
SCM Corporation
All rights reserved.
Printed and bound in the United States of America.

Published by Ideals Publishing Corporation
Nashville, Tennessee 37214
Published simultaneously in Canada

®The Durkee Logo is a Trademark of The SCM Corporation;
Ideals Publishing Corporation, Licensee.

All recipes were developed and tested in the
Durkee Kitchens, SCM Corporation.

Assorted spices and herbs

Spice and Herb Basics

Today, across the United States, there is a lively interest in spices and their uses. People everywhere are experimenting with spices and happily discovering what delicious variety they bring to foods. The popularity of ethnic foods has increased the usage of colorful and exotic spices while interest in tasty diet foods has revealed the low-sodium, low-calorie and low-cholesterol virtues of spices.

This fascination with spices, however, is not new—it is centuries old. The same spices that we take for granted have greatly influenced history. When prehistoric man wrapped meat in leaves to keep it clean, he discovered a means of seasoning food. Exactly where this first took place, no one knows, for spices are native to many lands. Wars have been fought to acquire certain spices. The Queen of Sheba gave King Solomon spices in tribute to his great wisdom. Marco Polo returned to Venice from the Orient with tales of sampling ginger in China, cinnamon in Ceylon, cloves and nutmeg in Molucca, and pepper in India. Columbus journeyed westward in search of a better route for spice trading.

Spices were almost impossible to obtain in colonial America; however, herbs were grown for everyday use. During the twentieth century, availability of spices from all over the world increased dramatically, as is indicated by the vast array of spices, herbs and blends now carried at the local supermarkets.

CLASSIFICATION OF SPICES

As a general rule, just about all the products found on the spice shelf of the supermarket are known as *spices*. According to the American Spice Trade Association, the word *spice* refers to any dried plant product used primarily for seasoning food. Spices, however, can be divided into the following categories:

True Spices come from the bark, roots, leaves, stems, buds, seeds or fruits of aromatic trees and plants which grow mainly in tropical countries. Spices are dried and available both whole and ground. Pepper, Allspice, Cloves, Nutmeg, Mace, Cinnamon, Ginger, Saffron and Turmeric are classified as true spices.

Herbs are the leaves and stems of soft, succulent plants which usually grow in a more temperate climate. They may be used fresh or dried; most are available whole and ground, and some are available in crushed form. Well-known herbs include Oregano, Marjoram, Mint, Basil, Parsley, Rosemary, Sage, Tarragon, Thyme and Bay Leaf.

Aromatic Seeds come from spices and herbs cultivated in both tropical and temperate areas. Sesame, Poppy, Celery, Cardamom and Coriander are typical.

Blends can include spices, herbs and seeds. Examples are Chili Powder, Curry Powder, Poultry Seasoning, Bonne Saveur, and Apple Pie Spice.

Dehydrated Vegetable Seasonings are dehydrated flakes, chips or powders of distinctively flavored vegetables such as Onion, Garlic, Parsley, Sweet Pepper and Chili Pepper.

BUYING AND STORING SPICES

- Buy only the amount of any product that you can use within its recommended storage time.
- Always buy the freshest-appearing packages and/or products, and record the date of purchase on the container.
- Store spices in a cool, dry place. Do not store over a stove or near an exhaust. Heat robs ground seasonings of their flavor, and dampness cakes and deteriorates powders.
- Keep spices away from sunlight, preferably in a dark place.
- To retain bright color and freshness, store red spices (chili powder, paprika, red pepper) in the refrigerator. Oily seeds like poppy and sesame are also best kept refrigerated.
- Store spices in airtight containers and close tightly after each use.

Under good conditions, seasonings retain their flavor and aroma for quite a long time. Whole spices keep longer than ground spices. Herbs tend to lose flavor a little faster than such items as pepper, ginger, cinnamon and cloves.

Ground spices and herbs may be given a "sniff test" once a year. This is done by quickly passing an opened container of the seasoning under the nose to determine if its contents can be identified. If not, discard and replace.

COOKING WITH SPICES
Amount to Use:
Since the pungency and the effect on different foods of each seasoning varies, it is not possible to

generalize about quantities to use. For the most satisfactory results, follow the recipe, measure the seasoning accurately and taste the food to adjust the seasoning for your preference.

If there is no recipe to follow, start with about one-fourth teaspoon of the seasoning for every pound of meat or pint of liquid. When adding strong-flavored seasoning such as Red Pepper or Garlic Powder, begin with a very small amount.

Add to these starter amounts according to your taste; however, remember, it is simple to add more seasoning and nearly impossible to subtract it. The art of seasoning foods is an endless adventure in new taste sensations. Properly used, seasonings will enhance the natural flavor of foods, not mask them.

When to Add:
Whole spices are best in long-cooking recipes and should be added at the beginning in order to allow the heat and moisture to release their flavor.

Ground spices may be added at the beginning and/or near the end of cooking. Ground spices added at the beginning of cooking gradually release flavor and add a mellow, subtle taste to the food. Adding ground spices during the last ten minutes of cooking will give a noticeable burst of flavor.

BASIC TIPS

- Familiarize yourself with the flavor and aroma of one new spice at a time. Try a single spice in a simple recipe (salad dressing, seasoned butter or basic sugar cookie) before combining with other spices.
- Combine Ground Mustard or Dehydrated Horseradish with an equal amount of water and allow to stand ten minutes to develop full flavor before using.
- If Instant Minced Onion or Garlic is being stirred into food with a large amount of liquid, there is no need to rehydrate. When sautéing minced onion or garlic, rehydrate in an equal amount of water.
- To prevent caking, do *not* shake or pour seasonings, especially onion and garlic, into steaming food; instead measure the amount and stir into the food.
- For easy removal of whole spices from the food being prepared, tie them in a cheesecloth bag before they are added.
- For quick flavor-release from leafy herbs, crush the herb in the palm of your hand or in a mortar with a pestle until finely crumbled.
- If spices are to be used in an uncooked recipe such as salad dressing, prepare the food ahead of time to allow flavors to blend.

- When using Sesame Seed as a garnish or incorporating into a recipe, toast lightly in a 350° oven, approximately 8 to 10 minutes.
- Substitute White Pepper for Black Pepper in any recipe where black specks may be undesirable, such as in a White Sauce.
- When reducing salt in a recipe, increased amounts of spices may be used. Black Pepper and Garlic are especially effective in replacing salt.
- Use seasoning blends like Fried Chicken, Lemon Fish or Broil 'n Grill to improve the flavor and appearance of microwaved foods.
- Do not be afraid to experiment with familiar spices in new ways. For instance, try a dash of Black Pepper in spice cake, Caraway Seed in apple pie crust or Apple Pie Spice in baked squash or sweet potatoes.

USEFUL EQUIVALENTS

- Generally, one teaspoon ground or crushed spice equals one tablespoon fresh spice.
- One-eighth teaspoon Garlic Powder or Instant Minced Garlic equals one clove garlic.
- One teaspoon Instant Onion (minced, chopped, diced) equals one tablespoon chopped fresh onion.
- One tablespoon Onion Powder equals one medium onion.
- One teaspoon Parsley Flakes equals two teaspoons minced fresh parsley.
- One teaspoon dried Grated Lemon or Grated Orange Peel equals one teaspoon fresh grated peel.
- Ten Whole Cardamom (pods removed and brown seeds crushed) equal one-half teaspoon Ground Cardamom.
- One-half teaspoon Ground Celery Seed equals one teaspoon Whole Celery Seed.
- One Whole Nutmeg equals two to three teaspoons Ground Nutmeg.
- One Whole Bay Leaf equals one-eighth to one-sixteenth teaspoon Ground Bay Leaves.
- One tablespoon Imitation Bacon Bits equals one slice bacon.
- One tablespoon Arrowroot equals one tablespoon cornstarch.

THE BASIC SPICE SHELF

Black Pepper	Oregano
Garlic Salt or Powder	Basil
Instant Minced Onion	Parsley Flakes
Onion Salt or Powder	Bay Leaf
Cinnamon	Seasoned Salt
Cloves	Paprika
Nutmeg	Poultry Seasoning
Chili Powder	Ground Mustard

Appetizers and Beverages

Herbed Cheese Spread

Makes 2 cups.

- ½ cup sour cream
- 1 8-ounce package cream cheese, softened
- ¼ cup Durkee Freeze-Dried Chives
- ¼ cup Durkee Parsley Flakes
- 2 teaspoons Durkee Leaf Thyme, crumbled
- ½ teaspoon salt
- ¼ teaspoon Durkee Garlic Powder
- Fresh vegetables *or* crackers

Cream together sour cream and cream cheese. Add chives, parsley flakes, thyme, salt and garlic powder; blend well. Chill at least 1 hour. Serve with vegetables or crackers.

Liver Paté

Makes 2 cups.

- 1 pound chicken livers
- 2 tablespoons butter *or* margarine
- ½ cup beef bouillon
- 3 tablespoons Durkee Instant Minced Onion
- 1 teaspoon Durkee Leaf Marjoram, crumbled
- ½ teaspoon salt
- ½ teaspoon Durkee Ground Thyme
- ¼ teaspoon Durkee Ground Celery Seed
- ¼ teaspoon Durkee Garlic Powder
- ⅛ teaspoon Durkee Ground Bay Leaves
- 1 3-ounce package cream cheese, softened
- 1 tablespoon milk
- Dash Durkee Ground Celery Seed
- Durkee Parsley Flakes

Sauté chicken livers lightly in butter. Add bouillon and next 7 ingredients; simmer until liver is barely firm, stirring frequently. Spoon mixture into blender container; blend until smooth. Chill. Beat cream cheese, milk and ground celery seed until smooth. Mound paté in serving bowl; cover with cream cheese mixture. Garnish with parsley flakes.

Spicy Fruit Dip

Makes 1½ cups.

- 1 12-ounce container lowfat cottage cheese
- 1 16-ounce can pineapple chunks, well drained
- 1 teaspoon Durkee Anise Seed, crushed
- Assorted fresh fruits

Place cottage cheese, ⅔ cup of the pineapple chunks and anise seed in blender; blend for 2 minutes or until smooth. Chop remaining pineapple and stir into dip. Serve with assorted fresh fruits.

Guacamole

Makes 2⅔ cups.

- 2 cups (about 2 large) chopped avocados
- 1 medium tomato, peeled, seeded and chopped
- 1 tablespoon lemon juice
- 1 tablespoon lime juice
- 1 tablespoon olive oil
- 1 teaspoon Durkee Ground Coriander
- ¾ teaspoon Durkee Onion Powder
- 2 green chilies, chopped
- ¼ teaspoon salt
- ¼ teaspoon Durkee Chili Powder
- ⅛ teaspoon Durkee Ground Black Pepper
- ⅛ teaspoon Durkee Garlic Powder

Combine all ingredients in mixing bowl; blend thoroughly. Chill 1 hour.

Bonne Saveur Dip

Makes 1½ cups.

- 1 cup sour cream
- ¼ cup mayonnaise *or* salad dressing
- 1 teaspoon Durkee Bonne Saveur Seasoning
- 1 teaspoon Durkee Chervil
- ¼ cup chopped nuts
- Crackers, chips, pretzels *and/or* fresh vegetables

Combine first 5 ingredients; blend thoroughly. Chill. Serve with dippers of your choice.

Party-Stopper Spinach Dip

Makes approximately 3 cups.

- 2 10-ounce packages frozen chopped spinach, thawed
- 1 cup mayonnaise
- 1 cup sour cream
- 3 tablespoons Durkee Instant Minced Onion
- 1½ tablespoons lemon juice
- 1 tablespoon Durkee Dill Weed
- 1 teaspoon salt
- ¼ teaspoon Durkee Freeze-Dried Chives
- ¼ teaspoon Durkee Parsley Flakes
- ¼ teaspoon Durkee Tarragon, crumbled
- ¼ teaspoon Durkee Leaf Thyme, crumbled
- Fresh vegetables

Drain spinach; squeeze out excess moisture and cut up finely with kitchen shears or sharp knife. Combine all ingredients; mix well. Cover and refrigerate 24 hours. Serve with fresh vegetables.

Clockwise, from top: Spicy Fruit Dip wi[th] assorted fresh fruits; Guacamole; Liver Pa[té]

Appetizers and Beverages

Brunswick Liver Paté

Makes approximately 1¾ cups.

   1 tablespoon Durkee Instant Minced Onion
   2 tablespoons lemon juice
   1 tablespoon Durkee RedHot! Sauce
   8 ounces braunschweiger
   6 tablespoons butter *or* margarine, softened
   2 tablespoons Durkee Parsley Flakes
   ¼ teaspoon Durkee Dill Weed
     Rye melba rounds *or* cocktail rye bread

Combine onion, lemon juice and hot sauce; let stand 10 minutes. Cream together braunschweiger and butter. Add onion mixture, 1 tablespoon parsley flakes and dill weed; mix well. Form into a smooth round on serving platter. Sprinkle with remaining parsley flakes. Serve with rye melba rounds or cocktail rye bread.

Apples with Cheese Dip

Makes approximately ¾ cup.

   1 8-ounce package cream cheese, softened
   ¼ cup light cream
   1 tablespoon Durkee Crystallized Ginger
   1 tablespoon Durkee Grated Orange Peel
   1 tablespoon salted peanuts
   2 unpeeled apples, sliced

Place all ingredients except apples in blender; blend until creamy. Serve with apple slices.

Pot-Bellied Mushrooms

Makes 24.

  24 large fresh mushrooms, about 1 pound
   ½ pound ground pork
   1 3-ounce package cream cheese, softened
   ¼ cup (1 ounce) shredded mozzarella cheese
   1 teaspoon Durkee Italian Seasoning
   ½ teaspoon salt
   ¼ teaspoon Durkee Fennel Seed, crushed
   2 tablespoons grated Parmesan cheese
   1 tablespoon Durkee Italian Parsley

Preheat oven to 350°. Wash and dry mushrooms; remove stems and chop fine. Brown pork in skillet over moderate heat; drain. Combine mushroom stems, pork, cream cheese, mozzarella cheese, Italian seasoning, salt and fennel seed; mix well. Stuff each mushroom cap with about 1 tablespoon filling. Place stuffed mushrooms in ungreased 10 x 15-inch jelly-roll pan. Top with Parmesan cheese and parsley. Bake 20 minutes.

Ham and Cheese Onyums

Makes 25 2-inch squares.

   1 13¾-ounce package hot roll mix
   4 tablespoons Durkee Freeze-Dried Chives
   1 cup mayonnaise
   4 cups (1 pound) shredded Swiss cheese
 1⅓ cups (about 5 ounces) diced cooked ham
   ½ teaspoon Durkee Curry Powder
   ½ teaspoon Durkee Garlic Powder
   1 2.8-ounce can Durkee French Fried Onions

Preheat oven to 375°. Prepare hot roll mix as directed on package, adding 2 tablespoons of the chives. Cover and let rise in warm place until doubled in size, 30 to 45 minutes. Pat dough into greased 10 x 15-inch jelly-roll pan. Combine mayonnaise and next 4 ingredients; blend well. Spread over dough in pan. Bake 25 minutes or until bubbly. Sprinkle top with crumbled French fried onions and remaining 2 tablespoons chives; bake 5 minutes. Cut into squares.

Barbecued Cocktail Meatballs

Makes approximately 50.

   1 pound ground pork
   1 pound ground beef
   2 tablespoons Durkee Chili Powder
   1 tablespoon Durkee Ground Cumin
   ½ teaspoon Durkee Leaf Thyme, crumbled
   ½ teaspoon Durkee Seasoned Salt
   ¼ teaspoon Durkee Garlic Powder
   ¼ teaspoon Durkee Ground Black Pepper
   2 cups barbecue sauce

Preheat oven to 300°. Combine all ingredients except barbecue sauce; mix well. Shape into 1-inch balls. Bake in ungreased 8 x 12-inch baking dish 20 minutes. Serve in heated barbecue sauce.

Rumple Scrumskins

Makes 8 servings.

   1 package (about 24 ounces) frozen potato thins,
     potato planks *or* steak fries
     Durkee Seasoned Salt
   1 cup (4 ounces) shredded Cheddar cheese
     Durkee Bacon Bits
   1 cup sour cream
   2 tablespoons Durkee Freeze-Dried Chives

Prepare potatoes according to directions; remove from oven. Sprinkle with seasoned salt, cheese and bacon bits. Combine sour cream and chives; blend well. Serve with potatoes.

Sizzlers

Makes 18 to 36 servings.

> 1 cup (4 ounces) shredded mozzarella cheese
> ¼ cup mayonnaise or salad dressing
> ¼ cup Durkee Bacon Chips
> ¼ cup chopped pimiento-stuffed Durkee Spanish Olives
> 1 teaspoon Durkee Italian Seasoning
> ½ teaspoon Durkee Fennel Seed, crushed
> 18 slices party rye bread

Combine all ingredients except bread; mix well. Cut bread slices in half, if desired. Spread mixture on bread. Broil 4 inches from heat until cheese melts and is lightly browned, about 4 minutes.

Crusty Italian Pitas

Makes 4 to 6 servings.

> 2 pita bread rounds
> 3 tablespoons butter or margarine, softened
> ½ teaspoon Durkee Imported Oregano, crumbled
> ½ teaspoon Durkee Sweet Basil, crumbled
> ¼ teaspoon Durkee Garlic Salt
> ¼ cup grated Parmesan cheese

Preheat oven to 400°. Separate each pita bread round into two thin layers by slicing through seam with sharp knife. Combine butter, oregano, basil and garlic salt; blend well. Spread mixture on unbrowned side of each round. Sprinkle each with 1 tablespoon Parmesan cheese. Arrange on ungreased baking sheet; bake 8 to 10 minutes. Break into halves or fourths.

Spicy Pickled Fish

Makes 6 servings.

> 2 pounds fish fillets
> 1 medium onion, sliced
> ½ cup white vinegar
> ⅓ cup vegetable oil
> ¼ cup dry white wine
> ¼ cup water
> 2 tablespoons sugar
> 1 tablespoon Durkee Pickling Spice
> 1 teaspoon salt

Preheat oven to 375°. Bake fish, covered, in ungreased 8 x 12-inch baking pan 20 minutes or until fish flakes easily; cool. Cut fish into chunks. Layer fish and onion slices in ungreased 2-quart casserole. Combine remaining ingredients in small saucepan and bring to a boil; boil 3 minutes. Let cool. Pour over fish and onion. Cover and refrigerate 24 hours; spoon liquid over fish occasionally.

Oriental Chicken Bites

Makes approximately 35.

> 2 whole chicken breasts, halved, skinned and boned
> 2 eggs
> 1 tablespoon vegetable oil plus ½ cup
> ½ teaspoon salt
> ¼ teaspoon Durkee Ground Black Pepper
> ¼ teaspoon Durkee Ground Ginger
> ¼ teaspoon Durkee Curry Powder
> ⅛ teaspoon Durkee Anise Seed, crushed
> ¾ cup dry bread crumbs
> ¾ cup finely chopped almonds
> Mustard Sauce (recipe on page 16)

Preheat oven to 425°. Cut chicken breasts into 3 x ½-inch pieces. Beat together eggs, 1 tablespoon vegetable oil, salt and spices. Combine bread crumbs and almonds in a shallow bowl. Spread remaining oil in two 10 x 15-inch jelly-roll pans (¼ cup per pan). Dip chicken pieces in egg mixture, 1 at a time; coat with bread crumb mixture. Place in pans. Bake 15 minutes or until tender. Serve with Mustard Sauce.

Crisp Lasagna Chips

Makes approximately 9 dozen.

> 1 16-ounce package lasagna noodles
> Vegetable oil
> ½ teaspoon salt
> 1 teaspoon Durkee Italian Seasoning*

Prepare lasagna noodles according to label directions, omitting salt; drain well. Diagonally cut each lasagna noodle into 2-inch pieces. Heat 1 inch vegetable oil to 375° in electric skillet. Fry cooked lasagna until golden brown on both sides; drain well on paper towels. Place salt and Italian seasoning in a medium-size plastic bag; add lasagna and shake until coated.

*Or substitute 1 teaspoon of any one of the following: Durkee Curry Powder, Durkee Lemon Flavored Pepper, Durkee Chili Powder or Durkee Paprika.

Variations:

Omit salt and Italian seasoning and substitute 1 teaspoon of any one of the following: Durkee Herb Vegetable Seasoning, Durkee Butter Salt, Durkee Celery Salt, Durkee Hickory Salt or Durkee Seasoned Salt.

Omit salt and Italian seasoning and substitute 1 tablespoon sugar and ½ teaspoon of any one of the following: Durkee Ground Cinnamon, Durkee Ground Cloves, Durkee Ground Allspice or Durkee Ground Ginger.

Zesty Cocktail Nuts

Makes approximately 4 cups.

- ¼ cup butter *or* margarine
- 2 teaspoons Durkee Hickory Salt
- 2 teaspoons Durkee Chili Powder
- 1 teaspoon Durkee Curry Powder
- ¼ teaspoon Durkee Ground Black Pepper
- 2 tablespoons Worcestershire sauce
- ½ teaspoon Durkee RedHot! Sauce
- 1 pound (about 4 cups) pecans, walnuts *and/or* almonds

Preheat oven to 300°. Melt butter in 9 x 13-inch baking pan. Add hickory salt, chili powder, curry powder, pepper, Worcestershire sauce and hot sauce; mix well. Add nuts, stirring until well-coated. Bake 30 minutes; stir every 10 minutes.

Harvest Popcorn

Makes 2½ quarts.

- ⅓ cup butter *or* margarine, melted
- 1 teaspoon Durkee Dill Weed
- 1 teaspoon Durkee Lemon Flavored Pepper
- 1 teaspoon Worcestershire sauce
- ½ teaspoon Durkee Garlic Powder
- ½ teaspoon Durkee Onion Powder
- ¼ teaspoon salt
- 2 quarts popped popcorn
- 2 1½-ounce cans Durkee Potato Sticks
- 1 cup mixed nuts

Preheat oven to 350°. Mix butter, dill weed, lemon pepper, Worcestershire sauce, garlic powder, onion powder and salt; toss with remaining ingredients. Spread mixture in ungreased 10 x 15-inch jelly-roll pan. Bake 6 to 8 minutes, stirring once.

Dilly Carrots

Makes approximately 4 cups.

- 8 carrots, peeled and cut into julienne strips
- ½ cup water
- ¼ cup cider vinegar
- 1 teaspoon Durkee Tarragon, crumbled
- 1 teaspoon Durkee Dill Weed
- 1 teaspoon Durkee Seasoned Salt

Place all ingredients in medium saucepan. Bring to a boil; reduce heat and simmer, covered, 30 minutes or until tender-crisp. Chill several hours or overnight.

Quick Cheese Sticks

Makes 48.

- 1 11-ounce package piecrust mix
- 1 1⅛-ounce package Durkee Cheese Sauce Mix
- 1 tablespoon Durkee Caraway Seed*
- 5 to 6 tablespoons cold water

Preheat oven to 350°. Combine piecrust mix and cheese sauce mix; blend thoroughly. Add caraway seed. Sprinkle with water; toss lightly until dough forms a ball. Divide pastry in half; place on lightly floured board. Roll each half into a 9 x 12-inch rectangle. Cut each half into twelve 1-inch-wide strips; cut each strip in half. Twist each strip twice; place on ungreased baking sheet. Bake 15 to 20 minutes or until golden.

Microwave Directions: Microwave on High 4 minutes, turning after each minute. Times can vary depending on particular oven being used; check manufacturer's directions.

*May substitute any of the following: 2 tablespoons Durkee Bacon Bits or Sesame Seed or 1 tablespoon Durkee Poppy Seed, Celery Seed or Italian Seasoning.

Clams Casino

Makes 4 servings.

- 4 slices bacon, cut into ½-inch pieces
- 3 tablespoons finely chopped onion
- 3 tablespoons finely chopped green pepper
- 3 tablespoons finely chopped sweet red pepper
- 2 teaspoons Worcestershire sauce
- ½ teaspoon Durkee Leaf Thyme, crumbled
- ½ teaspoon Durkee Leaf Marjoram, crumbled
- ½ teaspoon Durkee Lemon Flavored Pepper
- ¼ teaspoon Durkee Imported Oregano, crumbled
- ¼ teaspoon Durkee Parslied Garlic Salt
- 1 cup butter, softened
- 16 clams on the half shell
- ⅓ cup dry bread crumbs

Fry bacon in skillet until crisp. Remove bacon; crumble and set aside. Drain all but 1 tablespoon drippings from skillet. Add onion, peppers, Worcestershire sauce and seasonings to drippings in skillet; sauté until vegetables are tender. Remove from heat; cool completely. Whip softened butter; blend in cooled onion mixture and crumbled bacon. Place 1 tablespoon of seasoned butter on each clam; sprinkle with bread crumbs. Bake in preheated 450° oven 10 minutes or until golden brown and bubbly.

ockwise, from top: Fragrant Spiced Tea, ge 13; Iced Light Orangeade, page 13; arkling Eggnog Punch, page 13; Spiced ennese Coffee, page 12; Winter Warm-Up, ge 12

Spice and Herb Cookbook 11

Appetizers and Beverages

Sugar and Spice Nuts

Makes approximately 2 cups.

    1 12-ounce can mixed nuts
    1 egg white, beaten until foamy
    1 cup sugar
    ½ teaspoon Durkee Ground Cloves
    ½ teaspoon Durkee Ground Cinnamon
    ½ teaspoon Durkee Ground Nutmeg
    ¼ teaspoon Durkee Curry Powder

Toss nuts with beaten egg white to coat evenly. Combine sugar and spices; toss with nuts. Spread in 2-quart shallow baking dish. *Microwave on High 6 to 7 minutes, stirring halfway through cooking time. Spread evenly on cookie sheet to cool. Store tightly covered.

*Conventional Oven Instructions: Preheat oven to 200°. Bake 3 hours, stirring halfway through baking time.

Sunshine and Spice Punch

Makes approximately 3 quarts or 16 6-ounce servings.

    1½ cups water
    ½ cup sugar
    3 Durkee Stick Cinnamon, broken
    1 teaspoon Durkee Whole Allspice
    ½ teaspoon Durkee Whole Cloves
    2½ cups water
    1 6-ounce can frozen orange juice concentrate
    1 6-ounce can frozen pineapple juice concentrate
    ¼ cup lemon juice
    1 32-ounce bottle ginger ale, chilled
    Ice ring

Combine first 5 ingredients in small saucepan. Simmer, covered, 20 minutes. Strain and chill. Pour 2½ cups water, fruit juice concentrates and lemon juice in blender container; blend until frothy. Pour spice mixture, fruit juice mixture and ginger ale over ice ring in punch bowl just before serving.

Winter Warm-Up

Makes 2 servings.

    2 cups tomato juice
    1½ teaspoons Durkee Chili Powder
    Dash Durkee Ground Bay Leaves
    Dash Durkee RedHot! Sauce

Combine all ingredients in saucepan; simmer 2 minutes, over low heat, stirring occasionally. Serve warm.

Fireside Buttered Rum

Makes 12 6-ounce servings.

    1 cup butter or margarine, softened
    ½ cup confectioners' sugar
    ½ cup packed brown sugar
    1 teaspoon Durkee Ground Cinnamon
    1 teaspoon Durkee Ground Nutmeg
    1 pint vanilla ice cream, softened
    1 1-ounce bottle Durkee Imitation Rum Flavor
    6 cups boiling water
    Durkee Stick Cinnamon, optional
    Durkee Ground Nutmeg, optional

Cream together butter, confectioners' sugar, brown sugar and spices. Beat in softened ice cream and rum flavor until smooth. Pour into a 4-cup freezer container; freeze. Mixture will not freeze solid. Place ¼ cup mixture in each mug. Add ½ cup boiling water to each; stir well. Garnish with stick cinnamon and a sprinkle of nutmeg, if desired.

Spiced Viennese Coffee

Makes 6 to 8 servings.

    Cold water
    Ground coffee
    8 Durkee Whole Cloves
    4 Durkee Stick Cinnamon, broken
    8 Durkee Whole Allspice
    2 tablespoons Durkee Chocolate Flavor
    2 tablespoons honey
    Whipped topping, for garnish
    Durkee Whole Nutmeg, freshly grated for garnish

Prepare 6 cups percolated coffee according to usual procedure, except add cloves, cinnamon and allspice with coffee to percolator basket. Brew. Remove percolator basket. Add chocolate flavor and honey to coffee. Pour into cups; garnish with whipped topping and freshly grated nutmeg.

Mulled Cranberry Syllubub

Makes 8 servings.

   1 quart cranberry juice cocktail
   1 18-ounce can pineapple juice
   3 Durkee Stick Cinnamon
   1 teaspoon Durkee Whole Allspice
   1 teaspoon Durkee Whole Cloves
      Dash Durkee Ground Nutmeg
   ½ teaspoon Durkee Imitation Orange Extract
   ½ teaspoon Durkee Imitation Lemon Extract
      Durkee Stick Cinnamon, for garnish

Combine first 6 ingredients in large saucepan. Bring mixture to a boil; reduce heat and simmer, covered, 20 minutes. Remove from heat; strain. Stir in extracts. Serve hot in mugs; garnish with stick cinnamon.

Mulled Wine

Makes 12 3-ounce servings.

   2 Durkee Stick Cinnamon, broken
   1 teaspoon Durkee Cardamom Seed, pods cracked
   1 teaspoon Durkee Whole Cloves
   ½ teaspoon Durkee Whole Allspice
   1½ cups water
   ½ cup sugar
   1 bottle (750 ML) rosé wine
      Lemon peel twists

Tie spices in cheesecloth bag. Simmer spices, water and sugar in a 2-quart saucepan until sugar dissolves. Add wine; simmer 20 minutes; *do not boil.* Serve hot with lemon peel twists.

Fragrant Spiced Tea

Makes 6 servings.

   1 quart boiling water
   2 tea bags
   4 Durkee Whole Cloves
   2 Durkee Stick Cinnamon
   1 teaspoon Durkee Grated Orange Peel
   ½ cup sugar
   ¼ cup lime juice
   ½ teaspoon Durkee Imitation Lemon Extract
   ½ teaspoon Durkee Imitation Orange Extract
   6 strips lemon peel, for garnish

Combine first 7 ingredients; bring just to boiling. Reduce heat; simmer, covered, 15 minutes. Strain. Stir in extracts. Serve hot with lemon peel.

Iced Light Orangeade

Makes 13 4-ounce servings.

   1 cup sugar
   1 cup water
   1 orange peel, cut in strips
   1 lemon peel, cut in strips
   2 Durkee Stick Cinnamon
   1 teaspoon Durkee Whole Cloves
   ½ teaspoon Durkee Whole Allspice
   3 cups ice water
   2 cups orange juice
   ¼ cup lemon juice
      Ice
      Durkee Whole Cloves, for garnish
      Orange slices, for garnish

Combine sugar, 1 cup water, orange and lemon peels and spices in saucepan; simmer 10 minutes. Strain; cool liquid. Combine liquid, 3 cups ice water, orange and lemon juices. Serve over ice. Garnish with clove-studded orange slices.

Sparkling Eggnog Punch

Makes 4½ quarts.

   6 eggs
   ¼ cup sugar
   ½ teaspoon Durkee Ground Cinnamon
   ¼ teaspoon Durkee Ground Nutmeg
   ¼ teaspoon Durkee Ground Ginger
   ¼ teaspoon Durkee Ground Cloves
   2 quarts orange juice, chilled
   ½ cup lemon juice, chilled
   2 teaspoons Durkee Almond Extract
   1 quart vanilla ice cream
   1 32-ounce bottle ginger ale, chilled
      Durkee Ground Nutmeg, optional

Beat eggs in large bowl until thickened. Add sugar and spices; beat well. Stir in orange juice, lemon juice and almond extract; set aside. Scoop vanilla ice cream into punch bowl; stir in ginger ale and egg mixture until well blended. Sprinkle with additional nutmeg, if desired.

Soups and Sauces

Italian Chicken Stew

Makes 4 to 6 servings.

    1 medium onion, chopped
    1 tablespoon vegetable oil
    1 28-ounce can whole tomatoes with liquid
    2 medium potatoes, peeled and diced
    1 teaspoon Durkee Sweet Basil, crumbled
    ½ teaspoon Durkee Garlic Salt
    ½ teaspoon Durkee Imported Oregano, crumbled
    ¼ teaspoon Durkee Ground Black Pepper
    1 10-ounce package frozen mixed vegetables
    1 cup (about 5 ounces) chopped cooked chicken

Sauté onion in oil in a 4-quart saucepan, over medium heat, until tender. Stir in tomatoes with liquid, potatoes and seasonings. Bring to a boil; reduce heat and simmer, covered, 10 minutes. Add vegetables and chicken; simmer, covered, 25 minutes.

Melon-Strawberry Soup

Makes 7 cups.

    5 cups (3 to 4 pounds) watermelon cubes
    1 quart fresh strawberries
    1 cup orange juice
    1 tablespoon lemon juice
    2 tablespoons cornstarch
    ½ cup sugar
    1¼ teaspoons Durkee Grated Lemon Peel
    ½ teaspoon Durkee Ground Cinnamon
    ½ teaspoon Durkee Ground Allspice
    ¼ teaspoon Durkee Ground Cardamom
    ¼ teaspoon Durkee Mace
    1½ cups buttermilk

Place ⅓ of the watermelon and strawberries in blender or food processor; puree. Strain into medium saucepan. Repeat with remaining melon and berries. Combine orange juice, lemon juice and cornstarch; stir into fruit mixture. Add sugar, lemon peel and spices. Heat, stirring constantly, until mixture comes to a boil; cook 1 minute or until thickened. Remove from heat; stir in buttermilk. Cover; chill at least 8 hours.

Note: Soup may be frozen if buttermilk is omitted. After thawing, stir in buttermilk and serve.

Italian Wedding Soup

Makes 6 to 8 servings.

       Meatballs (recipe below)
    3 13¾-ounce cans chicken broth
    1 cup water
    ½ cup thinly sliced carrots
    ½ cup thinly sliced celery
    ½ cup thinly sliced green onions
    ½ teaspoon Durkee Sweet Basil, crumbled
    ½ cup broken spaghetti, uncooked
    ½ pound escarole, chopped and cooked

Prepare Meatballs; set aside. Combine next 6 ingredients in large saucepan. Bring to boil. Reduce heat, cover and simmer until vegetables are almost tender. Add spaghetti, escarole and meatballs; simmer 10 minutes longer.

Meatballs

    ¾ pound ground beef, pork and veal mixture
    1 egg, beaten
    ¼ cup dry bread crumbs
    2 tablespoons grated Parmesan cheese
    1 tablespoon Durkee Parsley Flakes
    ¼ teaspoon Durkee Garlic Salt
    ¼ teaspoon Durkee Ground Black Pepper
    ¼ teaspoon Durkee Imported Oregano, crumbled
    1 tablespoon vegetable oil

Combine all ingredients, except oil; mix well. Form mixture into 50 small meatballs. Brown meatballs in hot oil; drain.

Texas-Style Chili

Makes 6 to 8 servings.

    2 pounds chuck steak, cut in ½ inch cubes
    2 tablespoons vegetable oil
    1 medium onion, chopped
    1 14½-ounce can whole tomatoes with liquid
    1 6-ounce can tomato paste
    ⅓ cup water
    ¼ cup Durkee RedHot! Sauce
    2 tablespoons Durkee Chili Powder
    1 teaspoon Durkee Imported Oregano, crumbled
    ½ cup (2 ounces) shredded Monterey Jack cheese

Brown meat in oil; drain. Add remaining ingredients except cheese; simmer 1½ hours, stirring occasionally. Garnish with cheese.

Soups and Sauces

Minestrone

Makes 8 to 10 servings.

- 1 cup Great Northern beans, uncooked
- 1 16-ounce can whole tomatoes with liquid
- 2 10½-ounce cans condensed beef broth
- 1 cup sliced carrots
- 1 cup chopped celery
- 3 tablespoons Durkee Instant Diced Onion
- ½ teaspoon Durkee Leaf Thyme, crumbled
- ½ teaspoon Durkee Leaf Marjoram, crumbled
- ½ teaspoon Durkee Sweet Basil, crumbled
- ¼ teaspoon Durkee Instant Minced Garlic
- ¼ teaspoon Durkee Ground Bay Leaves
- ¼ teaspoon Durkee Ground Black Pepper
- 1 cup shredded cabbage
- 2 cups water
- ½ cup ditalini or elbow macaroni, uncooked
- 2 medium zucchini, sliced

Cook beans according to package directions; reserve 1 cup bean liquid. Combine tomatoes, tomato liquid, beef broth, carrots, celery and seasonings in 8-quart kettle. Bring to a boil; reduce heat and simmer 30 minutes. Add cooked beans, 1 cup bean liquid, shredded cabbage and water; continue simmering 15 minutes. Add ditalini and zucchini; cook until tender.

Cheesy Corn Chowder

Makes 6 servings.

- 2½ cups diced potatoes
- 2 cups water
- 1 cup sliced carrots
- ½ cup sliced celery
- 1 tablespoon Durkee Instant Chopped Onion
- 2 teaspoons Durkee Bon Saveur
- ¼ teaspoon Durkee Ground Black Pepper
- 2 1-ounce packages Durkee White Sauce Mix
- 2 cups milk
- 1 17-ounce can creamed corn
- 2 cups (8 ounces) shredded Cheddar cheese

Combine potatoes, water, carrots, celery, onion, Bon Saveur and pepper in a 3-quart saucepan. Bring to a boil; reduce heat and simmer, uncovered, 10 minutes. Do not drain. Prepare white sauce according to basic recipe for medium white sauce using milk. Add white sauce, corn and 1½ cups cheese to undrained vegetable mixture. Simmer 4 to 5 minutes, stirring occasionally, until heated through. *Do not boil.* Serve garnished with remaining cheese.

Cool 'n' Refreshing Gazpacho

Makes 6 to 8 servings.

- 6 medium-large ripe tomatoes, peeled and coarsely chopped
- 1 large cucumber, coarsely chopped
- 1 large green pepper, coarsely chopped
- 2 tablespoons Durkee Instant Minced Onion
- ⅛ teaspoon Durkee Instant Minced Garlic
- ½ cup tomato juice
- 2 tablespoons lemon juice
- 1 tablespoon vinegar
- ½ cup sour cream
- ¼ cup vegetable oil
- 2 teaspoons Durkee Seasoned Salt
- 1 teaspoon Durkee Paprika
- ½ teaspoon Durkee Mill Grind Black Pepper
- ¼ teaspoon Durkee Ground Celery Seed
- ¼ teaspoon Durkee Dill Weed
  Dash Durkee Ground Red Pepper
- ½ teaspoon Durkee RedHot! Sauce
  Croutons
  Durkee Parsley Flakes

Place ½ each of the chopped tomatoes, cucumber and green pepper in blender container. Refrigerate remaining chopped vegetables until serving time. Add minced onion, garlic, tomato juice, lemon juice and vinegar to blender container. Blend on high until of smooth consistency. Add sour cream, oil, spices and hot sauce; blend until thoroughly combined. Chill at least 4 hours. Just before serving, stir reserved, chopped vegetables into pureed mixture. Add more tomato juice if soup is too thick. Serve in chilled bowls; garnish with croutons and parsley.

Mustard Sauce

Makes ⅔ cup.

- ¼ cup vinegar
- 2 tablespoons water
- 1 egg
- 1 tablespoon butter or margarine
- 1 tablespoon sugar
- 1½ tablespoons Durkee Ground Mustard
- ¼ teaspoon Durkee Seasoned Salt
- ¼ teaspoon Durkee Turmeric
- ⅛ teaspoon Durkee Ground Allspice
  Dash Durkee Ground Cloves

Place all ingredients in blender container or small mixing bowl. Blend or mix on high speed until smooth. Pour into small saucepan and cook over medium-high heat, stirring constantly, until mixture comes to a boil and thickens. Refrigerate any unused sauce.

Piquante Sauce

Makes 2 cups.

- 1 16-ounce can diced tomatoes in puree*
- 1 4-ounce can chopped green chilies
- 1 tablespoon Durkee Instant Minced Onion
- ½ teaspoon Durkee Imported Oregano, crumbled
- ¼ teaspoon Durkee Ground Red Pepper
- ¼ teaspoon Durkee Chili Powder
- ⅛ teaspoon Durkee Garlic Powder

Combine all ingredients in saucepan. Simmer over medium heat 5 to 10 minutes. Serve hot or cold with tortilla chips or over tacos or enchiladas.

*May substitute tomato puree.

Bearnaise Sauce

Makes 1 cup.

- 3 tablespoons white wine
- 1 tablespoon white vinegar
- 1½ teaspoons Durkee Tarragon
- 1 teaspoon Durkee Chervil
- 1 teaspoon Durkee Instant Minced Onion
- ¼ teaspoon Durkee Ground White Pepper
- 3 egg yolks
- 1 tablespoon lemon juice
- ¼ teaspoon salt
  Dash Durkee Ground Red Pepper
- ½ cup butter or margarine, melted

Combine wine, vinegar, tarragon, chervil, onion and pepper in small saucepan. Boil until mixture is reduced to 2 tablespoons; place in blender container. Add egg yolks, lemon juice, salt and red pepper. Blend 30 seconds or until combined. Turn blender to run at low speed; gradually add butter in a slow steady stream, blending until mixture is smooth and thickened.

Texas Hot Barbecue Sauce

Makes approximately 2 cups.

- 2 8-ounce cans tomato sauce
- ½ cup Durkee RedHot! Sauce
- ½ cup packed brown sugar
- 2 teaspoons Durkee Ground Cumin
- 2 teaspoons Durkee Ground Oregano
- 1 teaspoon Durkee Garlic Salt

Combine all ingredients thoroughly. Brush on beef, pork or poultry during last 10 minutes of broiling or grilling; turn and baste frequently. Or pour over meat or poultry and bake at 350° until done.

Note: For medium-hot sauce, use ¼ cup plus 2 tablespoons RedHot! Sauce. For extra-hot sauce, use ½ cup plus 2 tablespoons RedHot! Sauce.

Horseradish Sauce

Makes 1 cup.

- 1 tablespoon Durkee Dehydrated Horseradish
- 1 tablespoon water
- 1 tablespoon vinegar
- 1 1-ounce package Durkee White Sauce Mix
- 1¼ cups milk
- ½ teaspoon Durkee Ground Mustard
- ⅛ teaspoon salt
  Dash Durkee Ground Red Pepper

Combine horseradish, water and vinegar. Cover and let rehydrate 30 minutes. Prepare White Sauce Mix according to package directions, except use 1¼ cups milk. Stir in rehydrated horseradish, mustard, salt and red pepper. Serve with beef or pork.

Delicious Raisin Sauce

Makes 1½ cups.

- ½ cup water
- ½ cup raisins
- ⅓ cup currant or port-wine jelly
- ½ teaspoon Durkee Grated Orange Peel
- ⅛ teaspoon Durkee Ground Allspice
  Dash salt
- 1 tablespoon Durkee Arrowroot
- ⅓ cup orange juice

Combine all ingredients except arrowroot and orange juice in saucepan. Heat to boiling, stirring constantly; lower heat. Combine arrowroot and orange juice; stir into raisin mixture. Cook over medium-high heat until thickened and clear.

Orange Dessert Sauce

Makes approximately 2 cups.

- 1 cup sugar
- 2 tablespoons Durkee Arrowroot
- 1 teaspoon Durkee Grated Orange Peel
- ½ teaspoon Durkee Grated Lemon Peel
- 1½ cups water
- ¼ cup orange juice
- 1 tablespoon lemon juice
- 2 tablespoons chopped Durkee Crystallized Ginger
- 1 11-ounce can mandarin oranges, drained and chopped in large pieces

Combine sugar, arrowroot, orange and lemon peel in a saucepan; stir in water, orange juice and lemon juice. Cook over low heat, stirring constantly, until thick and clear. Remove from heat; stir in crystallized ginger and oranges. Blend well. Serve warm or cold.

Salads and Dressings

Sweet-Sour Spinach Salad

Makes 10 to 12 servings.

- 4 quarts spinach, torn into bite-size pieces
- 4 hard-cooked eggs, chopped
- 4 slices bacon, cut into ½-inch pieces
- 2 tablespoons packed brown sugar
- ¼ cup vinegar
- ¼ teaspoon Durkee Seasoned Salt
- ⅛ teaspoon Durkee Sweet Basil, crumbled
- ⅛ teaspoon Durkee Leaf Marjoram, crumbled
  Dash Durkee Ground Black Pepper
- 1 2.8-ounce can Durkee French Fried Onions

Place spinach and chopped eggs in serving dish. Fry bacon until crisp; drain on paper towels and reserve. Remove all but 2 tablespoons bacon drippings from skillet. Stir brown sugar, vinegar, salt, basil, marjoram and pepper into drippings in skillet. Heat just to boiling; stir in bacon. Heat until bacon is hot; pour over spinach. Add French fried onions. Toss and serve immediately.

Antipasto Salad

Makes 8 cups.

- ⅔ cup vinegar
- ⅔ cup vegetable oil
- 4 teaspoons Durkee Instant Chopped Onion
- 1 teaspoon sugar
- 1 teaspoon Durkee Garlic Salt
- ½ teaspoon Durkee Italian Seasoning
- ½ teaspoon Durkee Sweet Basil, crumbled
- ½ teaspoon Durkee Imported Oregano, crumbled
- ½ teaspoon Durkee Ground Black Pepper
- 4 cups (12 ounces) sliced mushrooms
- 1 16-ounce can whole carrots, drained
- 1 14-ounce can artichoke hearts, drained and quartered
- 1 cup diagonally sliced celery
- ½ cup pitted ripe olives, halved
- ½ cup pimiento-stuffed Durkee Spanish Olives
- 1 2-ounce jar sliced pimiento, drained
  Lettuce

Combine vinegar, oil, onion, sugar and seasonings in saucepan. Bring to a boil; reduce heat and simmer, uncovered, 10 minutes. Combine remaining ingredients except lettuce in large bowl. Pour in hot marinade; stir; cover. Chill several hours or overnight, stirring occasionally. Serve in lettuce cups.

Marinated Carrot Salad

Makes 8 servings.

- 1 pound carrots, sliced diagonally ¼-inch thick
- 1 cup chopped celery
- ¼ cup Durkee Instant Minced Onion
- 1½ teaspoons Durkee Celery Seed
- ¾ teaspoon Durkee Grated Lemon Peel
- ½ teaspoon Durkee Ground Ginger
- ⅛ teaspoon Durkee Paprika
- 1 cup sugar
- ½ cup vinegar
- ½ cup water
- ⅓ cup vegetable oil

Cook carrots in boiling salted water about 10 minutes or until tender-crisp; drain. Toss carrots with celery, instant onion, celery seed, lemon peel, ginger and paprika. Combine remaining ingredients in a small saucepan; bring to a boil, stirring often. Pour over vegetables. Cover and chill 8 to 10 hours or overnight. Serve with a slotted spoon.

Special Steak Salad

Makes 4 servings.

- 1 large head romaine
- ½ cup butter *or* margarine
- ¼ teaspoon Durkee Imported Oregano, crumbled
- ¼ teaspoon Durkee Sweet Basil, crumbled
- ⅛ teaspoon Durkee Garlic Powder
- 4 slices French bread, cut in ½-inch cubes
- 1 medium onion, sliced
- 1½ cups sliced mushrooms
- 1½ pounds sirloin steak, cut in ⅜-inch strips
- 1 teaspoon Durkee Seasoned Salt
- ½ teaspoon Durkee Cracked Black Pepper
- ⅓ cup grated Parmesan cheese
  Cherry tomatoes

Wash romaine leaves; dry well and refrigerate for several hours until crisp and chilled. Make a bed of the large romaine leaves on 4 well-chilled plates just before serving. Tear remaining leaves into bite-size pieces in a large bowl. Melt ¼ cup butter in skillet; add oregano, basil and garlic powder. Sauté bread cubes in seasoned butter until golden brown; remove from skillet. Place remaining ¼ cup butter, onion, mushrooms and steak in skillet. Sauté until steak is cooked to desired doneness; sprinkle with seasoned salt and cracked black pepper. Combine meat mixture and romaine pieces. Toss gently. Divide among serving plates. Sprinkle croutons and cheese over salads. Garnish with cherry tomatoes.

Salads and Dressings

Salad Valencia

Makes 6 servings.

- 1 quart bite-size pieces romaine lettuce
- 1 11-ounce can mandarin oranges, drained
- ½ cup halved pitted ripe olives
- 1 cup thinly sliced fresh zucchini
- 1 avocado, peeled and sliced
- 1 2.8-ounce can Durkee French Fried Onions
  Valencia Dressing

Combine all ingredients except French fried onions and Valencia Dressing in a salad bowl. Add ½ can onions and ⅓ cup dressing just before serving; toss gently. Garnish with remaining onions.

Valencia Dressing

Makes approximately 1¾ cups.

- 1 6-ounce can frozen orange juice concentrate, thawed
- ¾ cup vegetable oil
- ¼ cup vinegar
- 3 tablespoons sugar
- ½ teaspoon Durkee Ground Mustard
- ¼ teaspoon Durkee Seasoned Salt
- 2 teaspoons Durkee RedHot! Sauce

Combine all ingredients; blend well. Refrigerate unused dressing.

Spiced Cran-Apple Salad

Makes 6 to 8 servings.

- 2 envelopes unflavored gelatin
- ¼ cup cold water
- ¼ cup sugar
- 1 cup apple juice, heated to boiling
- 1 16-ounce can whole berry cranberry sauce
- 1 cup chopped unpared apple
- ½ cup chopped celery
- ¼ cup chopped walnuts
- 1 teaspoon Durkee Apple Pie Spice
- ¼ teaspoon Durkee Ground Cardamom
  Cheese Topping

Soften gelatin in cold water. Add sugar and apple juice, stirring until dissolved. Stir in remaining salad ingredients and pour into a 1-quart shallow pan. Chill until set. Spread Cheese Topping over salad. Refrigerate until serving time.

Cheese Topping

- 1 3-ounce package cream cheese, softened
- ½ cup sour cream
- 1 tablespoon sugar
- ½ teaspoon Durkee Grated Lemon Peel
- ¼ teaspoon Durkee Ground Ginger

Combine all ingredients; blend until smooth.

Spice 'n' Yogurt Fruit Strata

Makes 12 to 14 servings.

- 1 cup (8 ounces) plain yogurt
- ¼ cup honey
- 1 teaspoon Durkee Ground Cinnamon
- ½ teaspoon Durkee Ground Nutmeg
- ¼ teaspoon Durkee Grated Lemon Peel
- ¼ teaspoon Durkee Grated Orange Peel
- ⅛ teaspoon Durkee Ground Ginger
- ½ teaspoon Durkee Lemon Extract
- ½ teaspoon Durkee Orange Extract
- 8 cups fresh fruit of your choice*
- 1 cup sliced almonds

Combine yogurt, honey, spices and extracts; stir until well blended. Layer 2 cups of one fruit, ¼ of the yogurt sauce and ¼ of the almonds in a 2-quart glass bowl. Repeat layers using a different fruit for each layer. Cover and chill several hours.

Fruit Options: Choose four of the following fruits using 2 cups of each fruit selected: sliced or cut-up apples, pears, peaches, kiwi, bananas, plums, mandarin oranges, pineapple chunks, melon balls, blueberries or strawberries.

Hot German Potato Salad

Makes 8 to 10 servings.

- 6 slices bacon, cooked and crumbled, reserve drippings
- ½ cup sugar
- 3 tablespoons flour
- 2 teaspoons Durkee Seasoned Salt
- 1 teaspoon Durkee Caraway Seed
- ½ teaspoon Durkee Ground Mustard
- ¼ teaspoon Durkee Ground Black Pepper
- 1 cup cider vinegar
- 1 cup water
- 6 cups (about 7 medium) sliced cooked potatoes
- 1 tablespoon Durkee Freeze-Dried Chives
  Durkee Freeze-Dried Chives, for garnish

Combine sugar, flour, seasoned salt, caraway seed, mustard and pepper; stir into bacon drippings. Cook over medium heat to make a smooth paste, 1 to 2 minutes. Blend in vinegar and water; bring to a boil, stirring constantly. Boil 2 to 3 minutes, continuing to stir constantly. Remove from heat; gently stir in potatoes and chives. Let stand 3 to 4 hours to fully blend flavors or refrigerate overnight. Warm before serving. Serve garnished with crumbled bacon and freeze-dried chives.

Marjoram Tuna Salad

Makes 4 to 6 servings.

- ½ cup chopped celery
- ½ cup mayonnaise *or* salad dressing
- 1 tablespoon Durkee Instant Minced Onion
- 1 tablespoon lemon juice
- 2 teaspoons Durkee Leaf Marjoram, crumbled
- 1 teaspoon Durkee Bon Saveur
- ¼ teaspoon Durkee Mill Grind Black Pepper
- 2 6½-ounce cans tuna, drained and flaked
  Lettuce
  Durkee Paprika

Combine celery, mayonnaise, onion, lemon juice, marjoram, Bon Saveur, pepper and tuna; toss just enough to mix. Chill. Serve on lettuce; garnish with paprika.

Deluxe Italian Parmesan Dressing

Makes approximately 1½ cups.

- ¾ cup vegetable oil
- ⅓ cup white vinegar
- ¼ cup grated Parmesan cheese
- 1 tablespoon honey
- 1 teaspoon Durkee Parslied Garlic Salt
- ¾ teaspoon Durkee Imported Oregano
- ½ teaspoon Durkee Sweet Basil
- ¼ teaspoon Durkee Onion Salt
- ¼ teaspoon Durkee Ground White Pepper

Combine all ingredients in blender container; blend well. Cover and chill. Blend or shake just before serving.

Poppy Seed Dressing

Makes approximately 2 cups.

- ¾ cup vegetable oil
- ¼ cup white vinegar
- 1 tablespoon Durkee Instant Minced Onion
- 1 tablespoon sugar
- 2 teaspoons lemon juice
- 1 teaspoon salt
- ½ teaspoon Durkee Ground Mustard
- ⅛ teaspoon Durkee Ground Red Pepper
- 1 cup mayonnaise *or* salad dressing
- 2 tablespoons Durkee Poppy Seed

Combine oil, vinegar, onion, sugar, lemon juice, salt, mustard and red pepper in a bowl; beat 3 minutes. Add mayonnaise and beat 3 minutes longer. Stir in poppy seed.

Creamy Herb-Buttermilk Dressing

Makes approximately 2 cups.

- 1 cup buttermilk
- 1 cup mayonnaise
- 1 teaspoon Durkee Onion Powder
- 1 teaspoon Durkee Parsley Flakes
- ½ teaspoon Durkee Garlic Powder
- ½ teaspoon salt
- ¼ teaspoon Durkee Ground Thyme
- ⅛ teaspoon Durkee Ground Black Pepper

Combine all ingredients in small bowl; blend thoroughly. Cover and chill at least 1 hour before serving.

Honey-Celery Seed Dressing

Makes 1½ cups.

- ½ cup sugar
- 2 teaspoons Durkee Celery Seed
- 1¼ teaspoons salt
- 1 teaspoon Durkee Instant Minced Onion
- 1 teaspoon Durkee Ground Mustard
- 1 teaspoon Durkee Paprika
- ⅓ cup honey
- 1 tablespoon lemon juice
- 1 cup vegetable oil
- ⅓ cup vinegar

Combine dry ingredients in mixer bowl or blender jar; blend in honey and lemon juice. Pour ¼ cup oil slowly into mixture, beating constantly. Add vinegar; blend well. Slowly add remaining oil, beating constantly. Beat 2 minutes after all oil has been added. Chill.

Russian Dressing

Makes approximately 2 cups.

- ⅔ cup vegetable oil
- ½ cup catsup
- ¼ cup sugar
- 3 tablespoons lemon juice
- 2 tablespoons Worcestershire sauce
- 2 tablespoons vinegar
- 2 tablespoons water
- 2 teaspoons Durkee Italian Parsley
- 1 teaspoon Durkee Instant Minced Onion
- 1 teaspoon Durkee Celery Seed
- ½ teaspoon Durkee Paprika
- ½ teaspoon salt
- ¼ teaspoon Durkee Mill Grind Black Pepper

Combine all ingredients in blender container; blend well. Cover and chill. Blend or shake just before serving.

Vegetables

Microwaved Twice-Baked Herb Potatoes

Makes 8 servings.

> **4** medium baking potatoes, scrubbed
> **½** cup sour cream
> **½** cup milk
> **¼** cup butter *or* margarine
> **2** teaspoons Durkee Herb Vegetable Seasoning
> **¼** teaspoon salt
> **⅛** teaspoon Durkee Ground Black Pepper
> **½** cup (2 ounces) shredded Cheddar cheese
>   Durkee Herb Vegetable Seasoning, for garnish

Pierce potatoes several times with a fork; arrange potatoes at least 1 inch apart on paper towels in microwave oven. Microwave on High 12 to 14 minutes, or until still slightly firm. Let stand 5 to 10 minutes. Halve potatoes lengthwise; scoop out centers, leaving skins intact; mash with sour cream, milk, butter and seasonings. Beat with electric mixer until smooth and fluffy; spoon into potato skins. Arrange on serving plate. Microwave on High 2 to 4 minutes. Top each potato half with 1 tablespoon cheese and sprinkle with additional herb vegetable seasoning. Microwave on High 2 minutes or until cheese is melted. Times can vary depending on particular oven being used; check manufacturer's directions.

Savory Buttered Limas

Makes 6 servings.

> **1** medium onion, sliced and separated into rings
> **¼** cup butter *or* margarine
> **1** teaspoon Durkee Savory, crumbled
> **1** teaspoon salt
> **⅛** teaspoon Durkee Leaf Thyme, crumbled
> **2** 10-ounce packages frozen baby lima beans, cooked and drained
> **1½** cups (6 ounces) shredded Monterey Jack cheese

Preheat oven to 350°. Sauté onion rings in butter in medium-size skillet until tender. Remove from heat and add seasonings, lima beans and cheese; mix well. Pour into ungreased 1½-quart casserole and bake, uncovered, 15 minutes or until heated thoroughly.

Festival Vegetables

Makes 4 to 6 servings.

> **⅓** cup butter *or* margarine
> **1** 10-ounce package frozen broccoli spears, thawed and cut in ½-inch pieces
> **1** 10-ounce package frozen corn, thawed
> **3** tablespoons chopped sweet red pepper
> **1¼** teaspoons Durkee Sweet Basil, crumbled
> **½** teaspoon Durkee Garlic Salt
> **⅛** teaspoon Durkee Crushed Red Pepper
> **⅛** teaspoon Durkee Ground Black Pepper

Melt butter in large skillet. Add remaining ingredients; stir well. Simmer, covered, 8 to 10 minutes, stirring occasionally.

Anise Carrots

Makes 4 to 6 servings.

> **1** pound carrots, peeled and cut diagonally in ½-inch slices
> **2** tablespoons butter *or* margarine
> **1** teaspoon Durkee Anise Seed, crushed
> **¼** cup orange juice

Cook carrots in lightly salted water 10 to 12 minutes or until tender; drain. Add butter and anise seed; cook 1 minute. Stir in orange juice and heat thoroughly.

Zucchini Paisano

Makes 4 to 6 servings.

> **3** cups (about 1 pound) sliced zucchini
> **2** cups sliced mushrooms
> **3** tablespoons vegetable oil
> **1** 16-ounce can tomato bits in tomato puree
> **¾** teaspoon Durkee Sweet Basil, crumbled
> **¾** teaspoon Durkee Garlic Salt
> **1** 2.8-ounce can Durkee French Fried Onions
> **½** cup ricotta cheese
> **⅓** cup grated Parmesan cheese
> **¼** cup milk
> **1** egg, lightly beaten

Preheat oven to 375°. Sauté zucchini and mushrooms in oil in large skillet until tender-crisp, about 5 minutes; remove from heat. Stir in tomato puree, spices and ½ can French fried onions. Place in greased 1½-quart casserole. Combine cheeses, milk and egg; blend until smooth; spread over casserole. Bake, uncovered, 30 minutes. Top with remaining onions; bake 5 minutes longer.

Vegetables

Herbed Green Beans

Makes 3 to 4 servings.

　1　9-ounce package frozen green beans
　¼　cup butter *or* margarine
　1½　teaspoons Durkee Instant Minced *or* Chopped
　　　Onion, rehydrated
　1½　teaspoons Durkee Parsley Flakes
　½　teaspoon Durkee Celery Salt
　½　teaspoon Durkee Rosemary Leaves, crumbled
　¼　teaspoon Durkee Garlic Powder
　1　hard-cooked egg, sliced
　　　Pimiento

Prepare beans as directed on package. Melt butter in small saucepan over low heat. Add remaining ingredients except egg and pimiento. Pour sauce over cooked, drained beans. Garnish with egg slices and pimiento.

Microwave Instructions: Place beans in 1-quart casserole. Sprinkle with ½ teaspoon salt. Dot with butter; sprinkle with remaining ingredients except egg and pimiento. Microwave, covered, on High 10 minutes, stirring halfway through cooking time. Garnish with egg slices and pimiento. Times can vary depending on particular oven being used; check manufacturer's directions.

Italian Bean Bake

Makes 6 to 8 servings.

　1　pound Great Northern beans, washed
　6　cups water
　2　tablespoons butter *or* margarine
　1　tablespoon salt
　1　14½-ounce can whole tomatoes with liquid
　1½　cups chopped celery
　⅓　cup Durkee Instant Minced Onion
　¼　cup packed brown sugar
　1　tablespoon Durkee Parsley Flakes
　1½　teaspoons Durkee Italian Seasoning
　¼　teaspoon Durkee Instant Minced Garlic
　¼　teaspoon Durkee Fennel Seed, crushed
　¼　teaspoon Durkee Mill Grind Black Pepper
　½　cup grated Parmesan cheese
　½　cup (2 ounces) shredded mozzarella cheese

Cover beans with water; bring to a boil and boil 2 minutes. Remove from heat. Cover and let stand 1 hour. Add butter and salt. Bring to a boil over high heat; cover and reduce heat. Simmer 2 hours or until tender. Drain beans, reserving liquid. Measure bean liquid; add water if needed to make ⅔ cup liquid. Add to beans along with remaining ingredients, except cheeses. Bring to a boil; pour into greased 2-quart casserole. Bake, uncovered, in preheated 350° oven 50 minutes. Sprinkle with cheeses; bake 10 minutes longer.

Gingery Vegetables

Makes 6 to 8 servings.

　4　medium yellow summer squash, sliced
　1　large green pepper, sliced
　1　medium onion, sliced
　¾　cup sliced mushrooms
　¼　cup butter *or* margarine
　2　medium tomatoes, cut in eighths
　1½　teaspoons Durkee Seasoned Salt
　1　teaspoon Durkee Ground Ginger

Sauté squash, pepper, onion and mushrooms in butter in large skillet until tender-crisp. Stir in tomatoes, salt and ginger. Cover and simmer 5 minutes or until tomatoes are warmed thoroughly.

Mexicali Fries

Makes 4 to 5 servings.

　½　cup vegetable oil
　1　12-ounce package frozen French fries
　2　teaspoons grated Parmesan cheese
　1　teaspoon Durkee Paprika
　½　teaspoon Durkee Garlic Salt
　¼　teaspoon Durkee Chili Powder

Heat oil in a large skillet over medium-high heat. Carefully add frozen potatoes to form a single layer. Cook 5 to 8 minutes or until golden brown, turning frequently with a spatula. Remove with a slotted spoon; drain on absorbent paper. Combine Parmesan cheese, paprika, garlic salt and chili powder; sprinkle over fries.

Saffron-Creamed Mushrooms

Makes 4 to 6 servings.

　2　tablespoons butter *or* margarine
　2　tablespoons minced green onion
　4　cups (about ¾ pound) quartered mushrooms
　⅛　teaspoon Durkee Imported Saffron
　½　cup white wine
　1　cup heavy cream
　¼　teaspoon salt
　⅛　teaspoon Durkee Ground White Pepper

Heat butter in a large skillet on medium until bubbly; sauté onion. Add mushrooms; toss until coated with butter. Reduce heat to medium-low; cook mushrooms, covered, stirring occasionally for 10 minutes. Uncover and increase heat; boil until mushroom liquid is almost evaporated, about 5 minutes. Crush saffron in small bowl with back of spoon; stir in wine and cream. Add to mushrooms and boil until reduced slightly, about 5 minutes. Stir in salt and pepper. May be served as an accompaniment to seafood and/or rice.

Oregano Potatoes

Makes 4 to 6 servings.

2 tablespoons butter *or* margarine
2 tablespoons shortening
4 cups sliced potatoes
1 teaspoon Durkee Imported Oregano, crumbled
½ teaspoon Durkee Seasoned Salt
¼ teaspoon Durkee Onion Powder
¼ teaspoon Durkee Mill Grind Black Pepper

Melt butter and shortening in large skillet over low heat; add potatoes. Cook over medium heat until bottom layer of potatoes is brown; turn potatoes and cook until brown. Combine seasonings; sprinkle over potatoes. Toss gently.

Corn Combinage

Makes 6 to 8 servings.

4 tablespoons butter *or* margarine
4 medium-size zucchini, sliced thin
1¼ teaspoons Durkee Seasoned Salt
½ teaspoon Durkee Imported Oregano, crumbled
¼ teaspoon Durkee Ground Black Pepper
2 12-ounce cans Mexican-style corn

Melt butter in large skillet. Stir in zucchini and sprinkle with seasoned salt, oregano and pepper. Sauté, stirring occasionally, 5 minutes. Add corn. Cover; simmer 5 to 8 minutes or until heated thoroughly.

Vegetable Brunch Monterey

Makes 6 to 8 servings.

½ pound fresh broccoli
3 tablespoons butter *or* margarine
2 teaspoons Durkee Celery Seed
½ teaspoon Durkee Garlic Salt
½ teaspoon Durkee Dill Weed
⅛ teaspoon Durkee Ground Black Pepper
½ pound (4 medium) carrots, peeled and diced
1 small onion, diced
6 eggs
1¼ cups milk
4 cups (1 pound) shredded Monterey Jack cheese

Preheat oven to 350°. Break flowerets from broccoli stems and reserve; cut stems into ½-inch pieces. Sauté in melted butter in large skillet 2 minutes. Add celery seed, garlic salt, dill weed and pepper; cook over medium-low heat 5 minutes, stirring occasionally. Add carrots, onion and broccoli flowerets; cover and cook until tender, about 10 minutes, stirring occasionally. Beat eggs and milk in a large bowl; add vegetable mixture and 3 cups cheese. Pour into a lightly greased 9 x 13-inch baking dish and top with remaining cheese. Bake 30 to 35 minutes or until cheese is golden and knife inserted in center comes out clean.

Crunchy Scalloped Celery

Makes 6 servings.

3 cups diagonally sliced celery, ¼-inch thick
1 10-ounce package frozen peas, thawed and drained
1 8-ounce can sliced water chestnuts, drained
1 4-ounce can mushroom stems and pieces, drained
1 10¾-ounce can condensed cream of celery soup
1½ teaspoons Durkee Mint Leaves, crumbled
½ teaspoon Durkee Seasoned Salt
½ teaspoon Durkee Savory, crumbled
¼ teaspoon Durkee Leaf Thyme, crumbled
2 tablespoons butter *or* margarine, melted
½ cup dry bread crumbs

Preheat oven to 350°. Simmer celery in a small amount of water 5 minutes; drain. Combine celery, peas, water chestnuts, mushrooms and soup. Stir in 1 teaspoon mint, ½ teaspoon seasoned salt, ¼ teaspoon savory and ⅛ teaspoon thyme. Pour into ungreased 1½-quart casserole. Combine butter, bread crumbs and remaining ½ teaspoon mint, ¼ teaspoon savory and ⅛ teaspoon thyme; sprinkle over casserole. Bake, uncovered, 25 minutes.

Yam Apple Scallop

Makes 6 to 8 servings.

¼ cup packed brown sugar
2 tablespoons chopped pecans
1 teaspoon Durkee Ground Cinnamon
½ teaspoon Durkee Ground Nutmeg
½ teaspoon Durkee Ground Coriander
2 tablespoons sherry
2 tablespoons butter *or* margarine, melted
1 pound sweet potatoes, cooked *or* 1 pound canned sweet potatoes, drained and sliced ¼-inch thick
2 apples, cored, pared and sliced ¼-inch thick
1 8¼-ounce can crushed pineapple, drained

Preheat oven to 350°. Combine sugar, nuts and spices; set aside. Combine sherry and butter; set aside. Layer half each of the sweet potatoes, apples, pineapple, spice mixture and sherry mixture in ungreased 2-quart casserole; repeat layers. Bake, covered, 30 minutes. Uncover and bake 10 to 15 minutes longer.

Spice and Herb Cookbook 25

Bracciole

Makes 4 servings.

>Meat Filling (recipe below)
>Italian Sauce (recipe below)
>1 pound thin-sliced (bracciole cut) round steak
>2 tablespoons olive oil
>Pasta

Prepare Meat Filling and Italian Sauce; set aside. If bracciole-cut round steak is unavailable, pound round steak between waxed paper to ¼-inch thickness. Spread Meat Filling over round steak; roll from narrow end and tie string around each roll to secure. Brown meat rolls in olive oil in large skillet. Pour Italian Sauce over meat rolls. Bring to a boil; reduce heat and simmer, covered, 1½ to 2 hours. Turn meat rolls and stir sauce occasionally. Remove string; cut in serving-size pieces. Serve over pasta.

Meat Filling

>1 pound ground pork
>1½ cups chopped mushrooms
>½ cup chopped onion
>½ teaspoon Durkee Sweet Basil, crumbled
>½ teaspoon Durkee Imported Oregano, crumbled
>½ teaspoon Durkee Leaf Thyme, crumbled
>½ teaspoon salt
>¼ teaspoon Durkee Rosemary Leaves, crumbled
>¼ teaspoon Durkee Garlic Powder
>¼ teaspoon Durkee Ground Bay Leaves
>¼ teaspoon Durkee Fennel Seed, crushed
>⅛ teaspoon Durkee Ground Black Pepper
>2 tablespoons dry bread crumbs
>2 tablespoons grated Parmesan cheese
>1 egg, lightly beaten

Brown meat in large skillet; add mushrooms, onion and seasonings. Cook until meat is done. Remove from heat; stir in bread crumbs, Parmesan cheese and egg.

Italian Sauce

>1 28-ounce can tomato puree
>1 cup water
>1 tablespoon Durkee Mint Flakes, crumbled
>1 teaspoon Durkee Sweet Basil, crumbled
>1 teaspoon Durkee Imported Oregano, crumbled
>½ teaspoon Durkee Onion Salt
>¼ teaspoon Durkee Instant Minced Garlic
>⅛ teaspoon Durkee Ground Black Pepper

Combine all ingredients.

Veal Milano

Makes 4 servings.

>4 (about 1 pound) breaded veal cutlets, ¼ inch thick
>2 tablespoons olive oil
>1 8-ounce can tomato sauce
>1 6-ounce can tomato paste
>1 4-ounce can mushroom stems and pieces, with liquid
>½ cup red wine
>2 tablespoons Durkee Instant Minced Onion
>1 tablespoon Durkee Italian Seasoning
>½ teaspoon Durkee Ground Oregano
>¼ teaspoon Durkee Fennel Seed, crushed
>⅛ teaspoon Durkee Garlic Powder
>⅓ cup grated Parmesan cheese
>1 cup (4 ounces) shredded mozzarella cheese

Preheat oven to 350°. Brown veal cutlets on both sides in hot oil in large skillet. Place cutlets in shallow ungreased 2-quart baking dish; set aside. Combine remaining ingredients except cheeses in skillet. Simmer, covered, 20 minutes. Pour sauce over cutlets; sprinkle with Parmesan cheese. Bake, covered, 30 minutes. Top with mozzarella; bake, uncovered, 5 to 10 minutes or until cheese melts.

Honey Spiced Ham

Makes 16 to 18 servings.

>1 10- to 12-pound fully-cooked bone-in ham
>Durkee Whole Cloves
>½ cup honey
>¼ cup butter or margarine
>1 teaspoon Durkee Ground Cinnamon
>½ teaspoon Durkee Ground Nutmeg
>¼ teaspoon Durkee Ground Allspice

Preheat oven to 325°. Place ham, fat-side up, on rack in shallow roasting pan. Score ham in diamond pattern, making cuts ¼ inch deep. Insert 3 cloves in center of each diamond. Insert meat thermometer into center of thickest part of meat, making sure the point does not rest in fat or on bone. Bake, uncovered, 2½ hours or until temperature is 130°. Combine remaining ingredients; cook over medium heat, stirring constantly, until mixture comes to a boil. Remove meat thermometer from ham. Spread half of glaze over ham; bake 15 minutes. Spread remaining glaze over ham; bake 15 minutes longer. For easier slicing, let ham stand 20 minutes.

Meat

Lemon Steak au Poivre

Makes 4 servings.

- 1 tablespoon Durkee Lemon Flavored Pepper
- 1 2-pound sirloin steak, cut 1 inch thick
- 1 tablespoon butter *or* margarine
- ¼ cup brandy
- ¼ cup beef bouillon
  Durkee Italian Parsley

Rub lemon pepper over both sides of steak, pressing into meat surface. Melt butter in large heavy skillet. Cook steak over medium-high heat, 5 to 7 minutes on each side or to desired doneness. Remove steaks to hot platter; keep warm. Add brandy and bouillon to skillet. Bring to boil and simmer 2 minutes. Pour over steak. Garnish with sprinkling of parsley.

Herb-Grilled Steak

Makes 6 to 8 servings.

- 1 3- to 4-pound sirloin *or* porterhouse steak, 1 to 1½ inches thick
- 1 teaspoon Durkee Onion Salt
- ½ cup vinegar
- ¼ cup vegetable *or* olive oil
- ¼ teaspoon Durkee Leaf Thyme, crumbled
- ¼ teaspoon Durkee Tarragon, crumbled
- ¼ teaspoon Durkee Dill Weed
- ¼ teaspoon Durkee Leaf Sage, crumbled

Rub both sides of steak with onion salt. Combine remaining ingredients and pour over steak. Marinate at least 1 hour, turning occasionally. Grill or broil steak about 6 inches from the heat 15 to 20 minutes on each side, brushing frequently with herb marinade.

Spice-Crusted Ham

Makes approximately 15 servings.

- 1 5-pound canned ham
- 1⅓ cup packed brown sugar
- ¾ cup soft bread crumbs
- 2 teaspoons Durkee Ground Mustard
- ½ teaspoon Durkee Ground Cinnamon
- ½ teaspoon Durkee Ground Black Pepper
- ¼ teaspoon Durkee Ground Cloves
- ¼ cup pineapple juice

Preheat oven to 325°; bake ham 1 hour. Remove from oven and score. Combine sugar, bread crumbs and spices; add juice; mix to form a thick paste. Spread over the ham. Preheat oven to 350°; bake ½ hour or until browned. Baste with pan juices before slicing.

Salisbury Steak

Makes 4 servings.

- 1 pound ground chuck
- 1 egg, lightly beaten
- ¼ cup dry bread crumbs
- 1 medium carrot, peeled and grated (about ¼ cup)
- 1 tablespoon Worcestershire sauce
- 1 tablespoon Durkee Instant Minced Onion
- 1 teaspoon Durkee Steak Salt
- 1 cup beef broth *or* bouillon
- 2 English muffins, halved and toasted

Combine ground chuck, egg, bread crumbs, carrot, Worcestershire sauce and onion. Shape into 4 patties. Sprinkle ⅛ teaspoon steak salt on each side; press seasoning gently into beef. Brown in skillet, about 4 minutes each side for medium doneness; drain. Add beef broth and simmer, uncovered, 5 minutes. Serve patties on toasted muffins; top with beef broth.

Oven-Baked Ragout

Makes 6 to 8 servings.

- 2 to 2½ pounds cubed pork *or* lamb
- 2 tablespoons vegetable oil
- ¼ cup flour
- 1 13¾-ounce can chicken broth
- 1¼ cups dry white wine
- 3 tablespoons Durkee Minced Onion
- ½ teaspoon Durkee Seasoned Salt
- ½ teaspoon Durkee Instant Minced Garlic
- ½ teaspoon Durkee Rosemary Leaves, crumbled
- ¼ teaspoon Durkee Ground Black Pepper
- ¼ teaspoon Durkee Leaf Thyme, crumbled
- ¼ teaspoon Durkee Leaf Marjoram, crumbled
- 2 cups ¼-inch-thick carrot slices
- 1 10-ounce package frozen peas, thawed
- 6 slices bacon
- 2 cups sliced mushrooms
  Durkee Parsley Flakes

Preheat oven to 325°. Brown meat on all sides, ⅓ at a time, in hot oil in Dutch oven; remove. Add flour to Dutch oven; cook over medium heat, stirring and scraping bottom of pan, 2 minutes. Stir in chicken broth, 1 cup wine and seasonings; cook, stirring constantly, until mixture boils and thickens. Remove from heat; stir in browned pork. Cover and bake 1½ hours. Stir in carrots and peas; bake, covered, ½ hour longer or until carrots are tender. Fry bacon in large skillet until crisp; remove, crumble and set aside. Drain all but approximately 3 tablespoons drippings; sauté mushrooms in reserved drippings, about 3 minutes. Add remaining ¼ cup wine; simmer 3 to 5 minutes. Stir mushroom mixture into ragout. Garnish with reserved crumbled bacon and parsley flakes.

Barbecued Brisket

Makes 6 to 8 servings.

    1 4-pound beef brisket
    ½ teaspoon Durkee Celery Salt
    ½ teaspoon Durkee Seasoned Pepper
    ¼ teaspoon Durkee Garlic Powder
    ¼ cup liquid smoke
 1½ cups barbecue sauce
    1 cup catsup
    1 tablespoon Durkee Celery Seed
    2 tablespoons Durkee Instant Minced Onion
    ⅛ teaspoon Durkee Ground Bay Leaves

Preheat oven to 325°. Place brisket in baking pan; rub each side with celery salt, seasoned pepper and garlic powder. Pour liquid smoke over both sides of brisket. Bake, covered, 3½ hours. (Brisket may be refrigerated or frozen at this point and completed later.) Remove any excess fat from pan drippings. Combine barbecue sauce, catsup, celery seed, onion and ground bay leaves; pour over brisket. Gently stir to combine barbecue sauce and pan drippings. Bake, covered, 1 hour. Slice brisket across the grain; top with sauce.

Dressed-Up Liver

Makes 6 to 8 servings.

    ¼ cup butter *or* margarine
    1 cup chopped celery
    1 cup sliced mushrooms
    ½ cup chopped onions
    2 pounds calves liver, cut in julienne strips
    1 teaspoon salt
    1 teaspoon sugar
    ¾ teaspoon Durkee Ground (Rubbed) Sage
    ¾ teaspoon Durkee Tarragon, crumbled
    ¼ teaspoon Durkee Seasoned Pepper
    ⅛ teaspoon Durkee Ground Nutmeg
    ½ cup white wine
    2 tablespoons flour
    ¼ cup water
    2 tablespoons catsup
    ½ cup sour cream
    1 tablespoon Durkee Italian Parsley
       Rice *or* noodles, optional

Heat butter in large skillet; add celery, mushrooms and onions; cook until soft but not brown. Add liver to skillet; sauté, turning often, about 5 minutes. Add seasonings and wine; cook, covered, 5 minutes. Blend flour and water to make a smooth paste; stir flour mixture and catsup into skillet. Cook, stirring constantly, until gravy thickens and comes to a boil. Remove from heat; blend in sour cream. Garnish with parsley. Serve with hot rice or noodles.

Mustardy Short Ribs

Makes 4 to 6 servings.

 3 to 4 pounds beef short ribs
    1 teaspoon Durkee Whole Cloves
    1 teaspoon Durkee Whole Allspice
    1 Durkee Bay Leaf
       Water
    ⅓ cup vinegar
    ¼ cup honey
    2 tablespoons Durkee Ground Mustard
    ½ teaspoon Durkee Garlic Salt
    ½ teaspoon Durkee Tarragon, crumbled
    ¼ teaspoon Durkee Onion Powder
    ⅛ teaspoon Durkee Ground Black Pepper

Place short ribs in 8-quart Dutch oven; add cloves, allspice, bay leaf and enough water to cover. Bring to a boil; reduce heat and simmer, covered, 1½ to 2 hours or until ribs are just tender; drain. Combine remaining ingredients in small saucepan to make glaze. Bring to a boil; reduce heat and simmer, uncovered, 5 minutes, stirring to blend. Remove from heat. Place short ribs in broiler pan; brush with mustard glaze. Broil, 4 to 5 inches from heat, 10 to 15 minutes or until browned. Turn and brush with glaze often.

Creamy Lasagna

Makes 8 servings.

    1 pound ground beef
    1 pound ricotta cheese
    2 eggs
    1 cup grated Parmesan cheese
    2 cups medium white sauce
    2 teaspoons Durkee Sweet Basil, crumbled
 1½ teaspoons Durkee Garlic Salt
    1 teaspoon Durkee Imported Oregano, crumbled
    ½ teaspoon Durkee Ground Black Pepper
    1 8-ounce package lasagna noodles, cooked according to package directions
    2 cups (8 ounces) shredded mozzarella cheese
    1 4-ounce can mushroom stems and pieces, drained

Preheat oven to 350°. Brown ground beef; drain. Combine ricotta cheese, eggs and ½ cup Parmesan cheese; blend well. Combine white sauce, spices and remaining Parmesan cheese; stir to blend. Spread a thin layer of white sauce in a greased 9 x 13 x 2-inch baking dish. Layer with ½ each lasagna noodles, ricotta mixture, mozzarella cheese, mushrooms, ground beef and white sauce. Repeat layering, ending with white sauce. Bake, covered, 45 minutes. Let stand 15 minutes.

Sherried Anise Roast

Makes 6 servings.

- 2 tablespoons shortening
- 1 3- to 3½-pound beef chuck roast
- 1 1-ounce package Durkee Onion Gravy Mix
- 1½ cups water
- ¼ cup soy sauce
- ⅓ cup sugar
- 1 tablespoon Durkee Anise Seed, crushed
- 1 Durkee Stick Cinnamon
- ⅛ teaspoon Durkee Ground Nutmeg
- ¼ cup sherry

Melt shortening in a 4-quart Dutch oven. Add roast and brown on all sides. Combine remaining ingredients except sherry in a small bowl; pour over meat. Bring to a boil; reduce heat, cover, and simmer 3 to 3½ hours or until tender, adding sherry during last half hour of cooking.

Spiced Pork Roast 'n' Rice

Makes 4 to 6 servings.

- Orange Glaze (recipe below)
- ½ teaspoon Durkee Parslied Garlic Salt
- ⅛ teaspoon Durkee Ground Bay Leaves
- ⅛ teaspoon Durkee Mill Grind Black Pepper
- 1 3½- to 4-pound pork roast
- Orange Rice (recipe below)

Prepare Orange Glaze; reserve ½ cup for Orange Rice. Combine seasonings; rub into meat. Roast meat, uncovered, in preheated 350° oven 2 to 2½ hours or until done, basting with Orange Glaze every ½ hour. While meat is roasting, prepare and bake rice. Serve pork roast on a platter surrounded by Orange Rice.

Orange Glaze

- 1 cup orange juice
- 1 tablespoon Durkee Instant Minced Onion
- ¼ cup packed brown sugar

Combine all ingredients; stir well.

Orange Rice

- 2 cups cooked rice (⅔ cup uncooked)
- ½ cup reserved Orange Glaze
- ⅔ cup chopped celery
- ⅓ cup chopped walnuts
- ¼ cup dark raisins
- ½ teaspoon salt
- ½ teaspoon Durkee Ground Cinnamon
- ⅛ teaspoon Durkee Ground Bay Leaves
- ⅛ teaspoon Durkee Ground Cloves

Combine rice, reserved Orange Glaze and remaining ingredients. Pour into ungreased 1-quart casserole. Bake at 350°, covered, 25 minutes.

Crispy Corn Dogs

Makes 12.

- Vegetable oil for deep fat frying
- 1 cup flour
- ¾ cup yellow cornmeal
- 2 tablespoons sugar
- 2 tablespoons Durkee Ground Mustard
- 2 teaspoons baking powder
- 1 teaspoon Durkee Seasoned Salt
- ½ teaspoon Durkee Onion Powder
- ¼ teaspoon Durkee Garlic Powder
- ¼ teaspoon Durkee Ground Red Pepper
- 1 cup milk
- 1 egg, lightly beaten
- 2 tablespoons shortening, melted
- 10 frankfurters (about 1 pound)

Heat oil to 375°. Combine flour, cornmeal, sugar, ground mustard, baking powder and seasonings; add milk, egg and shortening. Mix until smooth. Pour batter into a tall glass. Put frankfurters on skewers. Dip franks, one at a time, in cornmeal batter. Fry in hot oil until golden brown. Drain on paper towels.

Variation: For hors d'oeuvres, cut frankfurters in thirds crosswise. Put on toothpicks, dip in cornmeal mixture and fry.

Pocketful o' Fun Sandwiches

Makes 6 to 8 servings.

- 1½ pounds ground lamb *or* beef
- 1 teaspoon Durkee Rosemary Leaves, crumbled
- 1 teaspoon Durkee Parslied Garlic Salt
- ½ teaspoon Durkee Onion Powder
- ½ teaspoon Durkee Imported Oregano
- ¼ teaspoon Durkee Ground Cumin
- ⅛ teaspoon Durkee Ground Black Pepper
- 1 1⅛-ounce package Durkee Taco Seasoning Mix
- ½ cup water
- 4 medium tomatoes, peeled and chopped
- 1 medium green pepper, chopped
- Pita bread rounds
- Shredded lettuce, optional
- Shredded Cheddar cheese, optional

Preheat oven to 350°. Combine ground lamb and spices; shape into 1-inch meatballs. Brown meatballs on all sides in large skillet; drain. Stir in taco mix, water, tomatoes and pepper; simmer 8 to 10 minutes. Warm pitas in oven 5 minutes. Cut pitas crosswise; fill pockets with lamb mixture. If desired, garnish with shredded lettuce and cheese. Serve immediately.

Meat

Pork Chops with Anise Stuffing

Makes 6 servings.

- 1 medium green pepper, chopped
- ½ cup chopped onion
- 3 tablespoons margarine
- 3 cups bread cubes (6 slices bread)
- ½ teaspoon Durkee Seasoned Salt
- ½ teaspoon Durkee Anise Seed, crushed
- ⅛ teaspoon Durkee Ground Black Pepper
- 1 8¾-ounce can whole kernel corn with liquid
- 6 pork chops

Preheat oven to 325°. Sauté green pepper and onion in margarine until golden. Remove from heat; add bread cubes, salt, anise and pepper. Drain corn; reserve 3 tablespoons liquid; add corn and reserved liquid to stuffing mixture. Place pork chops in ungreased 8 x 12-inch baking pan; top with stuffing. Bake, covered, 1¼ hours.

"Sweet" Italian Sausage

Makes 2 pounds.

- 2 pounds coarsely ground pork
- 1 tablespoon Durkee Parsley Flakes
- 2 teaspoons salt
- 2 teaspoons Durkee Paprika
- 1½ teaspoons Durkee Fennel Seed
- 1 teaspoon Durkee Garlic Powder
- ½ teaspoon Durkee Mill Grind Black Pepper
- ½ teaspoon Durkee Leaf Thyme, crumbled
- ¼ teaspoon Durkee Ground Allspice
- ⅛ teaspoon Durkee Ground Nutmeg
- ¼ teaspoon Durkee Ground Bay Leaves
  Sausage casings, optional

Combine all ingredients except casings; blend well. Sausage may be stuffed into casings, if desired, and tied with cord at regular intervals or form sausage into patties..

Note: For "hot" Italian sausage, add ½ to 1 teaspoon Durkee Crushed Red Pepper.

Mock Pastrami

Makes 6 to 8 servings.

- ¼ cup Durkee Mill Grind Black Pepper
- ½ teaspoon Durkee Ground Cardamom *or* Durkee Dehydrated Horseradish
- 1 3-pound sirloin steak, 1½ to 2 inches thick
- 1 teaspoon Durkee Paprika
- ½ teaspoon Durkee Garlic Powder
- 1 cup soy sauce
- ¾ cup vinegar

Combine pepper and cardamom; press into meat evenly on all sides. Place meat in deep dish. Com-
bine remaining ingredients; pour over meat. Refrigerate, covered, 24 hours, turning occasionally so all sides of meat are in marinade. Remove from refrigerator; let stand at room temperature 1 hour. Broil steak 6 inches from heat, 15 minutes on first side and 10 minutes on second side for rare or longer to desired degree of doneness. Brush frequently with marinade.

Tallerine

Makes 4 to 5 servings.

- 1 pound ground beef
- 1 28-ounce can whole tomatoes with liquid
- 1 8-ounce can tomato sauce
- 2 tablespoons Durkee Sweet Pepper Flakes
- 1 tablespoon Durkee Instant Minced Onion
- ½ teaspoon Durkee Sweet Basil, crumbled
- ½ teaspoon Durkee Imported Oregano, crumbled
- ¼ teaspoon Durkee Leaf Marjoram, crumbled
- ¼ teaspoon Durkee Leaf Thyme, crumbled
- ¼ teaspoon Durkee Garlic Powder
- 2 cups uncooked noodles
- ½ cup pimiento-stuffed Durkee Spanish Olives, sliced
- ⅔ cup (3 ounces) shredded Cheddar cheese

Brown ground beef in large skillet; drain. Add tomatoes with liquid, tomato sauce, seasonings and noodles. Simmer, covered, 20 minutes, stirring occasionally. Stir in olives; sprinkle cheese over top of meat mixture. Simmer, covered, 5 minutes longer.

Spicy Barbecued Ribs

Makes 4 to 6 servings.

- 4 pounds spareribs, cut in serving-size pieces
- ⅓ cup Durkee Instant Diced Onion
- 1 tablespoon salt
- 1 tablespoon Durkee Pickling Spice
- 1½ cups water
- 1 cup catsup
- ¾ cup chili sauce
- ¼ cup packed brown sugar
- 2 tablespoons Worcestershire sauce
- 1 tablespoon Durkee Celery Seed
- 1 teaspoon Durkee Ground Mustard
- ¼ teaspoon Durkee Garlic Powder

Place ribs in 8-quart Dutch oven; add onion, salt, pickling spice and enough water to cover ribs. Cover and parboil ribs 1 hour. Combine water, catsup, chili sauce, brown sugar, Worcestershire sauce and seasonings in small saucepan. Bring to a boil; reduce heat and simmer 5 minutes. Place ribs in ungreased 9 x 13 x 2-inch baking pan. Pour barbecue sauce over ribs. Bake in preheated 325° oven 1 hour or until tender. Turn ribs in sauce at least once during baking time.

Pizza Strata

Makes 6 servings.

- 12 slices white bread
- 4 ounces sliced salami, cut in strips
- 1½ cups (6 ounces) shredded mozzarella cheese
- ¼ cup diced green pepper
- 5 eggs
- 2 cups milk
- ½ teaspoon Durkee Imported Oregano, crumbled
- ½ teaspoon Durkee Sweet Basil, crumbled
- ½ teaspoon Durkee Garlic Salt
- ½ teaspoon Durkee Italian Seasoning, crumbled
- ¼ teaspoon Durkee Ground Black Pepper
- 1 medium tomato, sliced thin

Trim crusts from bread. Place 6 slices of bread in greased 7 x 12 x 2-inch baking dish. Layer salami, cheese and green pepper on top of bread. Top with remaining 6 slices of bread. Beat together eggs, milk and seasonings. Pour evenly over strata. Cover; refrigerate at least 1 hour or overnight. Bake, uncovered, in preheated 325° oven 55 minutes or until a knife inserted near center of strata comes out clean. Top with tomato slices; bake 5 minutes longer. Let stand 5 to 10 minutes. Cut into squares.

Pork-Fried Rice

Makes 6 to 8 servings.

- 2 tablespoons vegetable oil
- 1 pound ½-inch pork cubes
- ¼ cup soy sauce
- 2 cups sliced mushrooms
- 1 cup sliced celery
- 1 sweet red pepper, sliced
- ½ cup chopped green onions
- 3 cups cooked rice, chilled (1 cup uncooked)
- 1 teaspoon Durkee Ground Coriander
- ½ teaspoon Durkee Ground Ginger
- ¼ teaspoon Durkee Garlic Powder
- ⅛ teaspoon Durkee Ground Black Pepper
- 2 eggs, lightly beaten
- 1 6-ounce package frozen pea pods, thawed

Heat oil in large skillet or wok. Stir-fry pork cubes over medium-high heat until cooked, about 15 to 20 minutes. Add soy sauce, mushrooms, celery, red pepper, onions, rice and seasonings; stir-fry about 5 minutes. Pour eggs over rice; stir and lift 1 minute until eggs are cooked. Stir in pea pods; cook until heated through. Serve immediately.

Shish Kebobs

Makes 4 servings.

- 1 cup vegetable oil
- ½ cup white wine
- 2 teaspoons Durkee Seasoned Salt
- 1 teaspoon Durkee Ground Thyme
- 1 teaspoon Durkee Ground Coriander
- 1 teaspoon Durkee Mill Grind Black Pepper
- ½ teaspoon Durkee Ground Bay Leaves
- 1½ pounds loin or leg of lamb, cut in 1-inch cubes
- 16 large mushrooms
- 1 large green pepper, cut in 1-inch pieces
- 1 large red onion, cut in 1-inch pieces

Combine vegetable oil, wine and spices; add lamb and vegetables. Stir to coat with marinade. Refrigerate, covered, 12 hours or overnight; stir occasionally. Drain marinade from lamb and vegetables; reserve marinade. Skewer lamb, green pepper and onion on eight 8-inch metal skewers, beginning and ending with a mushroom. Broil 4 to 5 inches from heat about 20 minutes or to desired doneness. Turn and baste frequently.

Ham and Cheese Supreme

Makes 6 to 8 servings.

- 6 slices bread
- 1 2.8-ounce can Durkee French Fried Onions
- 2 cups (8 ounces) shredded Cheddar cheese
- 2 cups (8 ounces) chopped cooked ham
- 1 10-ounce package broccoli spears, thawed, drained and cut in 1-inch pieces
- 5 eggs
- 2 cups milk
- ½ teaspoon Durkee Ground Mustard
- ½ teaspoon Durkee Bon Saveur
- ¼ teaspoon Durkee Mill Grind Black Pepper

Preheat oven to 325°. Cut 3 slices bread into cubes; place in greased 8 x 12-inch baking dish. Top with ½ can French fried onions, cheese, ham and broccoli. Diagonally cut remaining bread slices in half. Arrange bread down center of casserole, overlapping slightly, crusted points all in one direction. Beat together eggs, milk and seasonings; pour over entire casserole. Bake, uncovered, 1 hour and 10 minutes until center is firm. Top with remaining onions; bake 5 minutes longer. Let stand 10 minutes before serving.

Poultry

Herb Baked Chicken with Noodles

Makes 4 to 6 servings.

    3 tablespoons butter *or* margarine, melted
    1 teaspoon Durkee Paprika
    1 teaspoon Durkee Bon Saveur
    ¾ teaspoon Durkee Leaf Marjoram, crumbled
    ½ teaspoon Durkee Grated Lemon Peel
    ½ teaspoon Durkee Mill Grind Black Pepper
 2½ pounds chicken pieces
    4 cups (8 ounces) broad egg noodles, uncooked
    1 cup chicken bouillon
    ¼ cup white wine
    1 tablespoon cornstarch
    ½ cup grated Parmesan cheese
    1 tablespoon Durkee Italian Parsley
       Durkee Paprika, for garnish

Preheat oven to 375°. Combine butter and seasonings. Arrange chicken pieces in a single layer in ungreased shallow baking dish; pour butter mixture over chicken. Bake, uncovered, 45 to 50 minutes, basting with juices every 15 minutes. Cook noodles in boiling salted water until just tender; drain. Remove chicken to a heated serving platter. Combine pan drippings, bouillon, wine and cornstarch in a saucepan. Bring to a boil, stirring constantly, until mixture is thickened and bubbly. Stir in noodles, cheese and parsley. Arrange in a ring around edge of chicken. Garnish with additional paprika if desired.

Tandoori Chicken

Makes 8 to 10 servings.

    8 to 10 chicken breasts, split (about 5 pounds)
    2 cups plain yogurt
    ⅓ cup cider vinegar
    2 tablespoons lime *or* lemon juice
    2 teaspoons Durkee Seasoned Salt
 1½ teaspoons Durkee Ground Coriander
    ½ teaspoon Durkee Crushed Red Pepper
    ½ teaspoon Durkee Mill Grind Black Pepper
    ½ teaspoon Durkee Ground Mustard
    ½ teaspoon Durkee Ground Ginger
    ½ teaspoon Durkee Chili Powder
    ⅛ teaspoon Durkee Instant Minced Garlic
       Durkee Paprika

Place chicken in close-fitting bowl. Combine remaining ingredients, except paprika, and mix well; pour over chicken. Turn to coat well with marinade. Refrigerate to marinate at least 12 hours. Place chicken breasts, skin-side down, on rack in ungreased shallow baking pan. Bake, uncovered, in preheated 325° oven 30 minutes. Turn chicken and bake 20 to 30 minutes longer, frequently basting with remaining marinade. Place on serving platter; garnish with paprika.

Microwave Instructions: Prepare recipe as directed except place marinated chicken in two 7 x 11-inch glass baking dishes; cover with plastic wrap. Bake each dish of chicken separately in microwave oven. Microwave on High 10 minutes; rotate dish; microwave 10 minutes longer. Times can vary depending on particular oven being used; check manufacturer's directions.

Stir-Fry Chicken

Makes 6 servings.

    ¼ teaspoon Durkee Garlic Powder
    ¼ cup soy sauce
    3 tablespoons vegetable oil
    3 tablespoons cornstarch
    ½ teaspoon salt
    3 whole chicken breasts, skinned, boned and
       cut in strips
    ½ cup chicken bouillon
    ¼ cup sherry
    1 tablespoon Durkee Italian Parsley
    ½ teaspoon Durkee Ground Ginger
    ⅛ teaspoon Durkee Ground Red Pepper
    3 cups sliced mushrooms
    8 to 10 green onions, chopped
    1 cup diagonally sliced celery
    1 6-ounce package frozen Chinese pea pods, thawed
       and drained
    2 medium tomatoes, cut in wedges
       Rice

Combine garlic powder, 1 tablespoon soy sauce, 1 tablespoon vegetable oil, 1 tablespoon cornstarch and salt; add chicken and mix well. Let stand 30 minutes. Combine remaining 3 tablespoons soy sauce and 2 tablespoons cornstarch; stir in chicken bouillon, sherry, parsley, ginger and red pepper; set mixture aside. Pour remaining 2 tablespoons oil into wok or large skillet; heat on medium 2 minutes. Add mushrooms, green onions, celery and pea pods; stir-fry 2 to 3 minutes or until vegetables are tender-crisp. Remove from wok; set aside. Add chicken to wok; stir-fry 3 minutes; return stir-fried vegetables to wok. Add bouillon mixture and tomatoes; stir-fry 3 minutes or until thickened and bubbly. Serve over rice.

Poultry

Chicken Marengo

Makes 4 to 6 servings.

    2 to 3 pounds cut-up chicken
    2 tablespoons olive oil
1½ cups sliced mushrooms
    1 29-ounce can tomato puree
    ½ cup Chianti wine
    ½ cup water
    ½ cup Durkee Instant Diced Onion
    1 teaspoon Durkee Parsley Flakes
    1 teaspoon Durkee Sweet Basil, crumbled
    ¾ teaspoon Durkee Leaf Thyme, crumbled
    ½ teaspoon Durkee Grated Orange Peel
    ¼ teaspoon Durkee Instant Minced Garlic
    1 Durkee Bay Leaf
    ⅓ cup sliced pimiento-stuffed Durkee Spanish Olives

Brown chicken in oil in large skillet; remove. Place mushrooms in skillet; sauté lightly. Add remaining ingredients, except olives; simmer 10 minutes. Return chicken to skillet; simmer, covered, 30 minutes or until chicken is tender. Add sliced olives; simmer 10 minutes. Remove bay leaf.

Paella

Makes 6 to 8 servings.

    ¼ teaspoon Durkee Saffron
    1 10¾-ounce can condensed chicken broth
    1 pound hot Italian sausage, cut in 2-inch pieces
    1 tablespoon olive oil
    2 whole chicken breasts, split
    1 large red pepper, chopped
    1 large green pepper, chopped
    ¾ cup chopped onion
    1 cup regular rice, uncooked
    1 16-ounce can whole tomatoes with liquid
    1 cup dry white wine
    2 Durkee Bay Leaves
    1 tablespoon Durkee Italian Parsley
    ½ teaspoon Durkee Leaf Thyme, crumbled
    ¼ teaspoon Durkee Garlic Powder
    ¼ teaspoon Durkee Ground Black Pepper
    ¼ teaspoon Durkee Seasoned Salt
    1 10-ounce package frozen peas, thawed
    1 dozen Little Neck clams, scrubbed

Crush saffron with back of spoon in small saucepan; add chicken broth and heat just to boiling. Remove from heat; set aside to steep. Sauté sausage in oil in large skillet 5 minutes. Add chicken breasts; cover and continue cooking 15 minutes. Stir in chopped peppers, onion and rice; sauté until onion is golden. Add tomatoes and liquid, wine, seasonings and saffron broth; cover tightly and cook over medium heat 20 minutes. Add peas and clams; cook, covered, 8 to 10 minutes longer or until clams are tender. Remove bay leaves.

Chicken Paprikash

Makes 4 to 5 servings.

    ⅓ cup flour
    2 teaspoons Durkee Seasoned Salt
    ½ teaspoon Durkee Ground Black Pepper
2½ to 3 pounds cut-up chicken
    ¼ cup vegetable oil
1½ cups water
    1 15-ounce can tomato puree
    2 tablespoons Durkee Instant Minced Onion
    2 tablespoons Durkee Paprika
    ½ teaspoon Durkee Poultry Seasoning
    ¼ teaspoon Durkee Ground Bay Leaves
    ½ cup sour cream
    Spätzle *or* noodles

Combine flour, 1 teaspoon seasoned salt and ¼ teaspoon pepper in a plastic bag. Place chicken pieces in bag, one at a time; shake to coat. Brown chicken in oil in large skillet over medium heat, about 15 minutes. Combine water, tomato puree, onion, paprika, poultry seasoning, bay leaves and remaining seasoned salt and pepper; pour over chicken and simmer, covered, 40 to 45 minutes or until meat is tender, turning chicken occasionally. Remove chicken from pan. Stir sour cream into tomato mixture; heat over low heat; *do not boil.* Spoon sauce over chicken. Serve with spätzle or noodles.

Chicken Elegante

Makes 4 servings.

    4 slices cooked ham
    4 slices (about 3 ounces) Swiss cheese
    1 small tomato, chopped
    4 chicken breast halves, skinned and boned
    2 tablespoons butter *or* margarine, melted
    ½ cup dry bread crumbs
    2 teaspoons Durkee Italian Parsley
1½ teaspoons Durkee Fried Chicken Seasoning

Place 1 ham slice, 1 cheese slice and approximately 1 tablespoon chopped tomato on each chicken breast. Roll up jelly-roll fashion. Brush chicken with butter; roll in mixture of bread crumbs and seasonings. Place seam-side down in 9-inch glass pie plate; cover. Microwave on Medium 11 to 12 minutes, rotating dish ½ turn halfway through cooking time. Allow to stand, covered, 5 minutes before serving. Times can vary depending on particular oven being used; check manufacturer's directions.

Note: May be baked, uncovered, in preheated 350° oven 40 to 45 minutes.

Oven Fried Chicken

Makes 6 servings.

    2 eggs
    3 tablespoons butter *or* margarine, melted
    1 cup cornflake crumbs
    1 tablespoon Durkee Italian Parsley
1½ teaspoons Durkee Fried Chicken Seasoning
    1 teaspoon Durkee Sweet Basil
    ¼ teaspoon Durkee Leaf Thyme
    ¼ teaspoon Durkee Leaf Marjoram
    ⅛ teaspoon Durkee Garlic Powder
2½ to 3 pounds cut-up chicken

Preheat oven to 375°. Beat together eggs and butter in a shallow bowl. In another shallow bowl, stir together cornflake crumbs and seasonings. Dip chicken pieces in egg mixture, then dredge in crumbs. Place in ungreased shallow baking dish; do not crowd. Bake 30 minutes. Gently turn; bake 25 to 30 minutes longer or until chicken is done.

Southern Fried Chicken

Makes 4 servings.

2½ to 3 pounds cut-up chicken
    1 cup flour
    2 teaspoons Durkee Seasoned Salt
    1 teaspoon baking powder
    ½ teaspoon Durkee Onion Powder
    ¼ teaspoon Durkee Ground Cinnamon
    ¼ teaspoon Durkee Ground Ginger
    ¼ teaspoon Durkee Garlic Powder
    ¼ teaspoon Durkee Ground Black Pepper
    1 egg, lightly beaten
    Vegetable oil

Wash chicken; pat dry on paper towels. Place dry ingredients in large plastic bag; shake to blend. Dip chicken pieces in egg; shake in bag to coat. Heat oil, 1 inch deep, in large heavy skillet until a drop of water sizzles. Fry chicken pieces, covered, 30 minutes or until tender, turning chicken every 8 minutes; drain on paper towels. Serve immediately or keep in warm oven until ready to serve.

Lemon Barbecued Chicken

Makes 4 servings.

2½ to 3 pounds cut-up chicken
    1 cup vegetable oil
    ¾ cup lemon juice
    1 tablespoon Durkee Seasoned Salt
    2 teaspoons Durkee Paprika
    2 teaspoons Durkee Onion Powder
    2 teaspoons Durkee Sweet Basil, crumbled
    2 teaspoons Durkee Leaf Thyme, crumbled
    ½ teaspoon Durkee Garlic Powder

Place chicken in a shallow pan. Combine remaining ingredients in a jar; cover and shake to blend. Pour over chicken; cover. Marinate in refrigerator several hours or overnight, turning occasionally. Barbecue chicken over hot coals 15 to 20 minutes on each side, basting often with marinade.

Savory Chicken-Stuffed Zucchini

Makes 6 to 8 servings.

    4 medium zucchini
1½ cups (about 8 ounces) chopped cooked chicken
    1 cup (2 slices) bread cubes
    1 tomato, peeled and chopped
    1 egg, lightly beaten
    2 teaspoons Durkee Instant Minced Onion
    1 teaspoon Durkee Savory, crumbled
    ½ teaspoon salt
    1 8-ounce can tomato sauce
    2 tablespoons olive oil
    ¼ teaspoon Durkee Sweet Basil, crumbled
    ⅓ cup (about 1½ ounces) shredded mozzarella cheese

Preheat oven to 350°. Slice zucchini in half lengthwise; scoop out pulp, leaving ¼-inch shell. Chop pulp; combine with chicken, bread cubes, tomato, egg, onion, savory and salt; stuff zucchini shells. Combine tomato sauce, oil and sweet basil; pour in ungreased 8 x 12-inch baking dish. Place stuffed zucchini in baking dish. Bake, uncovered, 20 minutes or until tender. Top with cheese; bake 5 minutes. Serve topped with tomato sauce.

Chicken Enchiladas

Makes 4 servings.

    1 8-ounce can tomato sauce
    1 3½-ounce can chopped green chilies
    ¾ cup water
    1 tablespoon flour
    1 tablespoon vegetable oil
    1 tablespoon vinegar
    ½ teaspoon Durkee Imported Oregano, crumbled
    ¼ teaspoon Durkee Ground Cumin
    ¼ teaspoon Durkee Ground Red Pepper
    ¼ teaspoon Durkee Garlic Powder
    2 cups (10 ounces) cubed cooked chicken
1½ cups (6 ounces) shredded Cheddar cheese
    8 flour tortillas

Preheat oven to 350°. Blend first 10 ingredients in saucepan until smooth; bring to a boil, stirring constantly. Reduce heat; simmer 2 minutes. Place ¼ cup chicken, 2 tablespoons cheese and 1 tablespoon sauce on each tortilla. Roll up and place seam-side down in a greased 9 x 12-inch baking dish. Spread remaining sauce over enchiladas. Top with cheese. Bake, covered, 20 minutes.

Poultry

Sesame Cornish Hens with Coriander Glaze

Makes 4 servings.

- ⅓ cup butter *or* margarine
- ⅔ cup chopped onion
- ⅔ cup chopped celery
- 3 cups cooked rice (1 cup uncooked)
- ⅓ cup Durkee Sesame Seed, toasted*
- 1 tablespoon Durkee Parsley Flakes
- 2 teaspoons Durkee Poultry Seasoning
- ¼ teaspoon Durkee Ground Black Pepper
- 4 Cornish hens
  - Melted butter *or* margarine
  - Coriander Glaze (recipe below)

Preheat oven to 350°. Melt ⅓ cup butter in skillet; add onion and celery; sauté until translucent. Stir in cooked rice, sesame seed, parsley flakes, poultry seasoning and black pepper. Stuff Cornish hens; truss. Place hens breast-side up on rack in shallow roasting pan. Brush with melted butter. Roast, uncovered, 30 minutes. Prepare Coriander Glaze; brush over hens. Continue baking 30 minutes longer, basting frequently. Serve any remaining glaze with hens.

*Spread sesame seeds in single layer on ungreased baking sheet; bake at 350° 8 to 10 minutes or until lightly browned. Stir once during baking.

Coriander Glaze

- ⅓ cup sugar
- 1 tablespoon cornstarch
- 1 teaspoon Durkee Ground Coriander
- ¼ teaspoon Durkee Grated Lemon Peel
- ¼ teaspoon Durkee Onion Powder
  - Dash Durkee Ground Black Pepper
- 1¼ cups orange juice

Blend sugar, cornstarch and seasonings in saucepan; stir in orange juice. Bring to a boil, stirring constantly. Reduce heat; simmer 2 to 3 minutes until thickened.

Turkey Baste

Makes enough to baste a 10-pound turkey.

- ½ cup butter *or* margarine, melted
- ¼ cup dry sherry
- 1 tablespoon honey
- ½ teaspoon Durkee RedHot! Sauce
- ½ teaspoon gravy browning sauce
- ½ teaspoon Durkee Tarragon, crumbled
- ½ teaspoon Durkee Dill Weed
- ¼ teaspoon Durkee Ground Ginger
- ¼ teaspoon Durkee Ground Cumin

Combine all ingredients; brush on turkey every 30 minutes of roasting time.

Old-Fashioned Stuffing

Makes approximately 6 cups.

- ½ cup butter *or* margarine, melted
- 3 cups diced celery
- 1½ teaspoon Durkee Poultry Seasoning
- ¾ teaspoon Durkee Seasoned Salt
- ¼ teaspoon Durkee Ground Black Pepper
- 2 2.8-ounce cans Durkee French Fried Onions
- 3 quarts day-old bread crumbs (about 24 slices)
- 2 to 3 cups chicken broth

Combine first 5 ingredients; toss with onions and bread. Moisten with broth until well mixed. Add more broth if moister stuffing is desired. Use to stuff chops, meat rolls or poultry; or bake separately in a baking dish in preheated 350° oven 45 minutes.

Microwave Instructions: Prepare recipe as directed; place in 7 x 11-inch or 9-inch square glass baking dish; microwave, covered, on High 10 to 12 minutes. Times can vary depending on particular oven being used; check manufacturer's directions.

Harvest Fruit Stuffing

Makes enough stuffing for 8- to 10-pound turkey.

- 4 tart apples, unpeeled and quartered
- ½ cup water
- ¼ cup packed brown sugar
- 2½ cups cooked, mixed dried fruit (apricots, peaches, pears and prunes)
- ½ cup sherry
- ¼ teaspoon Durkee Ground Cinnamon
- ¼ teaspoon Durkee Ground Nutmeg
- ¼ teaspoon Durkee Mace
- 1 to 1½ cups fresh bread crumbs (about 7 slices)

Simmer apples in water and brown sugar until just barely tender. Stir in remaining ingredients, adding bread crumbs to desired moistness. Stuff turkey lightly.

Fish and Seafood

Poached Salmon with Herb Cream Sauce

Makes 4 servings.

- 1 cup water
- ¼ cup dry white wine
- 2 Durkee Bay Leaves
- 2 teaspoons Durkee Instant Chopped Onion
- 1½ teaspoons Durkee Butter Flavored Salt
- ¼ teaspoon Durkee Whole Allspice
- ¼ teaspoon Durkee Peppercorns
- ¼ teaspoon Durkee Grated Lemon Peel
- 4 salmon steaks, ½-inch thick
- 1 cup finely chopped cucumbers
- 3 tablespoons butter or margarine
- 2 tablespoons flour
- ¾ teaspoon Durkee Tarragon Leaves
- ½ teaspoon Durkee Parsley Flakes
- ⅛ teaspoon Durkee Dill Weed
- ½ cup sour cream

Combine water, wine, bay leaves, onion, butter salt, allspice, peppercorns and lemon peel in large skillet; bring to a boil. Place salmon in skillet; reduce heat and simmer, covered, 8 to 10 minutes or until fish flakes easily. Remove fish to a warm platter; strain and reserve 1¼ cups fish cooking liquid; set aside. Sauté cucumbers in butter in skillet until golden; reduce heat and stir in flour. Heat until mixture is bubbly, stirring constantly. Gradually add fish liquid and remaining seasonings. Cook and stir until mixture is of medium thickness. Stir in sour cream; warm sauce but do not boil. Serve over salmon.

Seasoned Pan Fried Trout

Makes 2 servings.

- ¼ cup yellow cornmeal
- ¼ cup flour
- ½ teaspoon Durkee Celery Salt
- ¼ teaspoon Durkee Garlic Powder
- ¼ teaspoon Durkee Onion Powder
- ¼ teaspoon Durkee Dill Weed
- ⅛ teaspoon Durkee Ground Black Pepper
- 1 egg
- 1 pound fresh trout
  Vegetable oil for frying

Combine dry ingredients in shallow bowl. Beat egg in separate bowl. Dip fish into egg, then into cornmeal mixture, coating well. Heat ¼-inch oil in large skillet. Fry fish over medium heat until golden on both sides and fish flakes easily.

Mock Crab Salad

Makes approximately 2 cups.

- 1 pound frozen sole fillets
- 1 cup water
- 2 slices onion, about ¼-inch thick
- ½ cup chopped celery
- 2 tablespoons Durkee Instant Chopped Onion
- 2 to 3 tablespoons chopped dill pickle or sweet pickle relish
- ½ cup mayonnaise
- ½ teaspoon Durkee Seasoned Salt
- ¼ teaspoon Durkee Dill Weed

Place frozen fish fillets in 10-inch skillet or large saucepan; add water and onion slices. Bring to boil; reduce heat to low and simmer, covered, 8 to 10 minutes or until fish becomes opaque and flakes easily. Drain and flake fish. Combine fish, celery, chopped onion, pickles, mayonnaise and seasonings in bowl; chill thoroughly. Serve as salad, sandwich filling or appetizer.

Variations:

Main Dish Salad: Serve on salad greens or in tomato or avocado half. Garnish with sliced avocado, lemon wedges or hard-cooked eggs.

Grilled Sandwiches: Spread mixture evenly on 6 slices of bread; top each with a slice of American cheese and a slice of bread. Grill on both sides until cheese melts and sandwich is golden.

Open-Faced Sandwiches: Spread mixture evenly on 6 English muffin halves; top with sliced tomato and cheese slice. Broil until cheese begins to melt.

Dilled Shrimp Bake

Makes 3 to 4 servings.

- ½ cup mayonnaise
- ½ cup white wine
- 1 10¾-ounce can condensed cream of shrimp soup
- 1 cup (4 ounces) shredded Swiss cheese
- ½ teaspoon Durkee Dill Weed
- 1 cup (4 ounces) small shell macaroni, cooked and drained
- 1 4½-ounce can small shrimp, drained
- 1 2.8-ounce can Durkee French Fried Onions

Preheat oven to 350°. Blend together mayonnaise, wine, soup, cheese and dill weed. Stir in macaroni, shrimp and ½ can French fried onions; blend well. Pour into ungreased 1½-quart casserole. Bake, covered, 30 to 35 minutes. Top with remaining onions; bake, uncovered, 5 minutes longer.

Salmon Loaf with Lemon Butter Sauce

Makes 4 servings.

    1 cup cooked regular rice (⅓ cup uncooked)
    1 15½-ounce can red salmon, drained, skinned,
        boned and flaked
    ⅓ cup chopped onion
    ¼ cup chopped celery
    1 teaspoon Durkee Lemon Fish Seasoning
    ¼ teaspoon Durkee Dill Weed
        Dash Durkee Ground Black Pepper
    ½ cup milk
    1 egg, beaten
        Lemon Butter Sauce (recipe below)

Preheat oven to 350°. Combine cooked rice, salmon, onion, celery and seasonings. Combine milk and egg; blend with salmon mixture. Place in greased 3½ x 7½-inch loaf pan. Bake 1 hour or until firm. Serve with Lemon Butter Sauce.

Lemon Butter Sauce

Makes 1 cup.

    2 tablespoons butter
    2 tablespoons flour
    1 teaspoon Durkee Lemon Fish Seasoning
    1 cup milk

Melt butter in saucepan; blend in flour and seasoning. Add milk; bring to boil, stirring constantly. Reduce heat and cook until thickened, stirring constantly.

Tuna Rice Baskets

Makes 6 servings.

    1 cup rice, uncooked
    1 tablespoon Durkee Parsley Flakes
    1 teaspoon Durkee Dill Weed
    1 9¼-ounce can tuna, drained and flaked
    1 cup thin white sauce
    ¼ cup finely chopped carrots
    ¼ cup finely chopped celery
    1 tablespoon lemon juice
    1 teaspoon Durkee Poultry Seasoning
    ¼ teaspoon Durkee Ground Black Pepper
    1 2.8-ounce can Durkee French Fried Onions
    ¾ cup (3 ounces) shredded Cheddar cheese

Preheat oven to 350°. Prepare rice according to package directions; stir in parsley and dill. Spoon ½ cup rice into each of 6 greased 10-ounce custard cups; press evenly over bottom and up sides to form rice basket. Combine tuna, white sauce, carrots, celery, lemon juice, seasonings and ½ can French fried onions in large bowl; mix well. Spoon tuna mixture into rice baskets; bake, uncov-

ered, 15 minutes. Top each cup with cheese and remaining onions. Bake 5 minutes longer.

Stuffed Sole Hollandaise

Makes 3 to 4 servings.

    1 10-ounce package frozen chopped spinach, thawed
        and well drained
    2 tablespoons dry bread crumbs
    1 tablespoon grated Parmesan cheese
    1 egg, lightly beaten
    ½ teaspoon Durkee Tarragon, crumbled
    ¼ teaspoon Durkee Garlic Powder
    1 pound sole fillets, thawed if frozen
    1 1-ounce package Durkee Hollandaise Sauce Mix
    ⅔ cup milk
        Durkee Paprika

Preheat oven to 350°. Combine spinach, bread crumbs, cheese, egg and spices; mix well. Spoon mixture over fish and roll up; secure with toothpicks. Place in greased 9 x 12-inch baking dish. Prepare Hollandaise Sauce Mix according to package directions, using milk. Pour over fish; cover and bake 20 minutes or until fish flakes easily. Serve garnished with paprika.

Seafood Cream Curry

Makes 6 servings.

    2 tablespoons butter or margarine
    ½ cup chopped onion
    ⅓ cup finely chopped celery
    2 tablespoons flour
    4 teaspoons Durkee Curry Powder
    1 teaspoon salt
    ½ teaspoon Durkee Ground Ginger
    ¼ teaspoon Durkee Garlic Powder
    ⅛ teaspoon Durkee Ground Cumin
    ⅛ teaspoon Durkee Ground Red Pepper
    1½ cups milk
    1 cup heavy cream
    1 pound cooked sole fillets, cut into chunks
    1 6-ounce package frozen shrimp, cooked
    1 6-ounce package frozen crab meat, cooked
        Cooked rice

Melt butter in large skillet over low heat. Add onion and celery; cook until golden. Combine flour and seasonings; add to skillet and cook, stirring constantly, 3 minutes. Increase heat to medium; gradually add milk, stirring until smooth. Reduce heat to low; simmer 10 minutes. Blend in cream and seafood just before serving; heat through. Serve over hot rice.

Superb Broiled Halibut

Makes 4 servings.

- 4 teaspoons lemon juice
- 1 tablespoon water
- 1 teaspoon Durkee Salad Herbs
- ¼ teaspoon Durkee Ground Mustard
- ¼ teaspoon Durkee Onion Powder
- ⅛ teaspoon Durkee Ground Black Pepper
- ⅛ teaspoon Durkee Garlic Powder
- 4 halibut steaks (about 1½ pounds)
- Durkee Butter Flavored Salt
- 1 tablespoon olive oil

Combine lemon juice, water and seasonings; let stand 5 minutes. Arrange fish on greased broiler pan. Lightly sprinkle both sides of fish with butter salt. Add olive oil to herb mixture; baste fish. Broil 3 to 4 inches from heat 5 to 8 minutes or until light brown. Baste once with herb mixture. Turn fish carefully; baste with herb mixture. Broil 5 to 8 minutes longer or until fish flakes easily.

North Coast Kebobs

Makes 6 servings.

- Marinade (recipe below)
- 18 large shrimp
- 18 scallops
- 18 bacon slices, halved and partially cooked
- 18 mushroom caps
- 18 pineapple chunks
- 18 green pepper pieces
- 18 onion wedges

Prepare Marinade; pour over shrimp and scallops. Allow to marinate at least 2 hours. Skewer marinated seafood and remaining kebob ingredients alternately on twelve 8-inch skewers. Grill or broil, 4 to 5 inches from heat, 8 to 10 minutes or until done. Turn halfway through cooking; brush with marinade. Boil remaining marinade until mixture thickens; drizzle over cooked kebobs.

Marinade

- 3 tablespoons soy sauce
- 3 tablespoons dry white wine
- 2 tablespoons Worcestershire sauce
- 2 tablespoons vegetable oil
- 1 tablespoon liquid smoke
- 1 tablespoon packed brown sugar
- 1 teaspoon Durkee Ground Ginger
- 1 teaspoon Durkee Garlic Powder
- 1 teaspoon Durkee English-Style Ground Mustard
- ½ teaspoon Durkee Lemon Flavored Pepper
- ¼ teaspoon Durkee RedHot! Sauce

Combine all ingredients; mix well.

Monterey Dill Fillets

Makes 2 to 3 servings.

- 1 cup medium white sauce
- ½ teaspoon Durkee Dill Weed
- ½ teaspoon Durkee Bon Saveur
- ¼ teaspoon Durkee Onion Powder
- 1 pound fish fillets, thawed if frozen
- ½ cup (2 ounces) shredded Monterey Jack cheese
- 6 slices bacon, fried crisp, drained and crumbled

Preheat oven to 375°. Combine white sauce and seasonings. Place fillets in shallow baking dish; pour sauce over top. Bake, covered, 20 minutes. Sprinkle with cheese and bacon. Bake, uncovered, 5 minutes longer.

Lemony Herb Fish

Makes 2 to 3 servings.

- 1 pound fish fillets, thawed if frozen
- 1 tablespoon butter or margarine, melted
- 2 tablespoons grated Parmesan cheese
- ½ teaspoon Durkee Lemon Flavored Pepper
- ¼ teaspoon Durkee Imported Oregano, crumbled
- ¼ teaspoon Durkee Leaf Marjoram, crumbled
- ¼ teaspoon Durkee Savory, crumbled

Preheat oven to 375°. Place fillets in ungreased shallow baking dish; drizzle with melted butter. Combine remaining ingredients; sprinkle over fillets. Bake, covered, 20 to 25 minutes or until fish flakes easily.

Chervil Sole

Makes 2 to 3 servings.

- 1 pound sole fillets, thawed if frozen
- 1½ teaspoons Durkee Chervil
- 1 teaspoon Durkee Bon Saveur
- ¼ teaspoon Durkee Paprika
- 1 medium onion, sliced and separated into rings
- ½ cup chicken bouillon
- ¼ cup white wine
- 1 tablespoon lemon juice
- 2 tablespoons butter or margarine

Preheat oven to 350°. Place fillets in ungreased shallow 2-quart baking dish. Combine seasonings; sprinkle over both sides of fillets. Place onions over fillets. Combine bouillon, wine and lemon juice; pour over fish; dot with butter. Bake, uncovered, 20 to 25 minutes or until fish flakes easily.

Breads

Italian Fennel Bread Sticks

Makes 5 to 6 dozen.

      1 package active dry yeast
    ¾ cup warm water (110 to 115°)
      1 cup beer, room temperature
    ½ cup olive oil
      1 tablespoon Durkee Fennel Seed
    1½ teaspoons salt
      1 teaspoon Durkee Mill Grind Black Pepper
      1 teaspoon sugar
    4½ cups all-purpose flour
      1 egg, beaten with 2 tablespoons water
        Coarse salt
        Durkee Sesame Seed *or* Poppy Seed

Combine yeast and water; stir to dissolve yeast. Blend in beer, olive oil, seasonings and sugar; stir in enough flour to make a stiff dough. Turn onto floured surface; knead until dough is smooth and elastic. Place in lightly oiled bowl, cover, and let rise in warm place until double in size. Punch dough down; let rest, covered, about 5 minutes. Roll dough to ¼-inch thickness on lightly floured surface. Cut into strips about ¼ x 7-inches; gently roll or twist to about 8 inches. Place on lightly greased baking sheets. Brush lightly with beaten egg and water; sprinkle with coarse salt and one of the seeds. Bake in a preheated 350° oven 20 to 25 minutes until golden brown, turning over halfway through baking.

Note: To restore crispness after storing, place on ungreased baking sheets; heat at 350° about 10 minutes.

Dill-Pickle Rye Bread

Makes 2 round loaves.

      4 cups all-purpose flour
      2 packages active dry yeast
      1 cup water
    ½ cup dill pickle liquid
    ½ cup buttermilk *or* sour milk
    ¼ cup vegetable oil
      2 tablespoons sugar
      2 teaspoons Durkee Dill Seed
      2 teaspoons Durkee Caraway Seed
      1 teaspoon salt
      2 cups rye flour
      1 egg, beaten
        Durkee Caraway Seed, for garnish

Combine 2 cups all-purpose flour and yeast in large bowl of electric mixer. Heat water, pickle liquid, buttermilk, oil, sugar, seeds and salt in saucepan until warm (120°); pour over flour-yeast mixture; beat at medium speed about 3 minutes or until smooth. Stir in rye flour with wooden spoon; add remaining all-purpose flour; stir to make soft dough. Turn out onto lightly floured board; knead until smooth and elastic. Cover dough with mixing bowl; let rest 40 minutes. Punch down and knead again until smooth. Divide dough in half; shape in 2 smooth round balls; place each in a greased 1-quart round glass casserole. With sharp knife, cut three slits on loaf tops. Brush with egg; sprinkle with additional caraway seed. Let rise in warm place until double, about 40 minutes. Bake in preheated 350° oven 50 minutes, or until bread sounds hollow when tapped. If browning too quickly, cover loosely with foil last 10 minutes of baking. Cool in casseroles 10 minutes; turn out on rack to cool.

Create-Your-Own Muffins

Makes 12.

    1½ cups all-purpose flour
    ½ cup sugar
      2 teaspoons baking powder
    ½ teaspoon salt
      1 egg
    ½ cup milk
    ¼ cup vegetable oil
        Spices and fruits *or* cheese (Variations below)

Preheat oven to 400°. Stir together dry ingredients. Beat egg lightly; stir in milk and oil. Add to dry ingredients. Mix just until dry ingredients are moistened. Fold in favorite spices and fruit or cheese. Spoon into greased muffin cups, filling ⅔ full. Bake 20 to 25 minutes. Immediately remove from pan. Serve hot.

Variations:

Blueberry 'n' Spice: Fold 1 teaspoon Durkee Grated Lemon Peel, ½ teaspoon Durkee Mace, ½ teaspoon Durkee Ground Cinnamon and 1 cup blueberries into batter.

Spicy Apple-Raisin: Fold 1 cup grated apple, ¼ cup raisins and 1½ teaspoons Durkee Apple Pie Spice into batter.

Herb-Cheese: Fold ½ cup (2 ounces) grated cheese and 2 teaspoons Durkee Herb Vegetable Seasoning into batter.

Cherry Twist Wreath

Makes 1 large wreath, 10 to 12 servings.

1 package active dry yeast
½ cup warm milk (about 110°)
¼ cup warm water (about 110°)
¼ cup butter *or* margarine, softened
3 tablespoons sugar
1½ teaspoons salt
1 teaspoon Durkee Ground Cinnamon
1 teaspoon Durkee Grated Lemon Peel
½ teaspoon Durkee Almond Extract
3¼ to 3½ cups all-purpose flour
Spicy Cherry-Almond Filling (recipe below)
Sugar Glaze (recipe below)

Dissolve yeast in milk and water in large mixing bowl; blend in butter, sugar, salt, cinnamon, lemon peel and almond extract. Beat in 2 cups of the flour, 1 cup at a time, using mixer on medium speed. Beat 3 minutes; scrape bowl often. Beat in enough remaining flour (about 1¼ cups) with a heavy-duty mixer or wooden spoon to form a soft dough. Turn dough out onto floured surface; knead until smooth, 5 to 10 minutes. Turn dough over in a greased bowl, cover, and let rise in a warm place until double in size, about 1½ to 2 hours. Prepare, cover, and chill Spicy Cherry-Almond Filling. Punch dough down; turn out on a floured surface; roll out into a 9 x 30-inch rectangle. Crumble filling over dough; spread to within 1 inch of edges. Roll up jelly-roll fashion starting with long side. Pinch to firmly seal edges. Cut roll in half lengthwise with a floured knife; carefully turn cut sides up. Loosely twist together, keeping cut sides up. Transfer to greased and floured baking sheet. Shape into 10-inch circle; pinch ends together firmly to seal. Let rise, uncovered, in a warm place 45 to 60 minutes or until about double in size. Bake in preheated 375° oven 20 to 25 minutes or until browned. Transfer to rack to cool. Drizzle with Sugar Glaze while warm.

Spicy Cherry-Almond Filling

¼ cup soft butter *or* margarine
¼ cup flour
¼ cup sugar
1 cup finely chopped blanched almonds
⅓ cup chopped Durkee Red Maraschino Cherries
⅓ cup chopped Durkee Green Maraschino Cherries
½ teaspoon Durkee Ground Cinnamon
½ teaspoon Durkee Ground Nutmeg
½ teaspoon Durkee Grated Lemon Peel
⅛ teaspoon Durkee Ground Cloves
⅛ teaspoon Durkee Curry Powder

Beat together butter, flour and sugar with electric mixer. Stir in remaining ingredients; blend well.

Sugar Glaze

⅔ cup confectioners' sugar
1 tablespoon water
1 teaspoon lemon juice

Combine all ingredients; blend until smooth.

Quick Swedish Rye Bread

Makes 1 loaf.

1 13¾-ounce package hot roll mix
¾ cup warm water (110 to 115°)
2 eggs
1 tablespoon packed brown sugar
2 tablespoons light molasses
1 tablespoon Durkee Grated Orange Peel
2 teaspoons Durkee Caraway Seed
¾ cup rye flour
1 egg, beaten
Durkee Caraway Seed, for garnish

Dissolve yeast from hot roll mix in water in mixing bowl; stir in 2 eggs, brown sugar, molasses, orange peel and caraway seed. Combine flour from hot roll mix and rye flour; stir into yeast mixture. Dough will be sticky. Let rise according to package directions. Turn out onto floured surface; toss lightly to cover dough with flour. Shape into round loaf; place in greased 1½-quart casserole or 9-inch pie plate. Brush with beaten egg; sprinkle with additional caraway seed. Let rise according to package directions. Bake in preheated 350° oven 30 minutes. Remove from dish; cool on rack.

Orange Ginger French Toast

Makes 4 servings.

½ cup light corn syrup
¼ cup honey
3 tablespoons frozen orange juice concentrate
1¼ teaspoons Durkee Ground Ginger
1 11-ounce can mandarin orange segments, drained
4 eggs, beaten
1 cup milk
½ teaspoon salt
Butter *or* margarine
8 slices French *or* white bread

Combine corn syrup, honey, orange juice concentrate and ½ teaspoon ginger in small saucepan; bring to a boil. Stir in oranges; set aside and keep warm. Blend eggs, milk, remaining ¾ teaspoon ginger and salt in a shallow bowl. Melt butter over medium-high heat in a large skillet. Dip bread in egg mixture, coating both sides; place in skillet and cook 3 to 4 minutes on each side or until golden brown. Serve with warm orange sauce.

Golden Ginger Scones

Makes 12.

    2 cups all-purpose flour
    6 tablespoons sugar
 1½ tablespoons Durkee Grated Orange Peel
 2½ teaspoons baking powder
    2 teaspoons Durkee Ground Ginger
    ½ teaspoon baking soda
    ½ teaspoon salt
    ½ cup butter *or* margarine, softened
    1 egg
    ¾ cup buttermilk
    1 tablespoon finely chopped Durkee Crystallized
      Ginger

Preheat oven to 425°. Stir together flour, 4 tablespoons sugar, orange peel, baking powder, ginger, baking soda and salt in large bowl. Cut in butter with 2 knives or pastry blender until particles are fine. Beat together egg and buttermilk with fork; add to flour mixture; toss with fork to mix thoroughly. Divide in 2 parts; turn each onto heavily floured board; knead lightly with floured hands, pat in circle ⅝ inch thick and cut into 6 wedges with floured knife. Place wedges on ungreased cookie sheet; sprinkle with combination of remaining sugar and crystallized ginger. Bake 14 to 15 minutes or until golden.

Spiced Zucchini Bread

Makes 2 loaves.

    3 eggs
    1 cup vegetable oil
    1 cup sugar
    1 cup packed brown sugar
    1 tablespoon Durkee Imitation Maple Flavor
    2 cups coarsely shredded zucchini
 2½ cups all-purpose flour
    1 cup chopped walnuts
    ½ cup toasted wheat germ
    2 teaspoons baking soda
    1 teaspoon salt
    ½ teaspoon baking powder
    1 teaspoon Durkee Ground Cinnamon
    ½ teaspoon Durkee Mace
    ¼ teaspoon Durkee Ground Cloves
    ⅓ cup Durkee Sesame Seed

Preheat oven to 350°. Beat eggs with mixer; add oil, sugars and maple flavor; continue beating until mixture is thick and foamy. Stir in zucchini. Combine flour and remaining ingredients, except sesame seed; stir gently into mixture just until blended. Divide batter equally between 2 greased and floured 5 x 9 x 3-inch loaf pans. Sprinkle sesame seed evenly over the top of each. Bake 1 hour or until toothpick inserted in center comes out clean. Cool in pan 10 minutes; turn out on wire racks to cool.

Herbed Bubble Bread

Makes 10 to 12 servings.

    2 1-pound loaves frozen bread dough
    ¼ cup butter *or* margarine
    2 tablespoons grated Parmesan cheese
    1 teaspoon Durkee Leaf Thyme, crumbled
    ½ teaspoon Durkee Dill Weed
    ½ teaspoon Durkee Sweet Basil, crumbled
    ¼ teaspoon Durkee Rosemary Leaves, crumbled

Thaw bread dough in refrigerator overnight. Allow to rise at room temperature 1 hour. Knead both loaves into 1 ball; cut dough into 25 small pieces; shape into balls. Melt butter and add remaining ingredients; mix well. Dip dough balls into butter-herb mixture; place in greased bundt pan. Cover, let rise in warm place until doubled in size. Bake in preheated 350° oven 30 to 40 minutes. Cool 5 to 10 minutes; then loosen edges and remove from pan. Serve warm.

Coffee-Time Cardamom Braid

Makes 1 loaf.

    1 13¾-ounce package hot roll mix
    ¾ cup warm water (110 to 115°)
    2 tablespoons butter *or* margarine, melted
    1 egg, lightly beaten
    1 teaspoon Durkee Ground Cardamom
    ¼ teaspoon Durkee Grated Orange Peel
    ¾ cup golden raisins
      Orange Glaze (recipe below)

Soften yeast from package of roll mix in warm water; stir in flour from roll mix and remaining ingredients except Orange Glaze. Blend well. Cover with waxed paper; let rise in warm place (80°) until double, about 1 hour. Turn out onto floured board; knead 2 to 3 minutes. Divide dough into thirds; shape each part into a roll about 12 inches long. Arrange on greased baking sheet about 1 inch apart; braid loosely, from the middle; pinch ends together. Cover and let rise again until doubled, about 40 minutes. Bake in preheated 375° oven 25 to 30 minutes or until done. Spread with Orange Glaze while hot.

Orange Glaze

    ½ cup confectioners' sugar
    1 tablespoon milk
    ¼ teaspoon Durkee Grated Orange Peel

Stir together all ingredients.

*ockwise, from top: Create-Your-Own Muffins, page 44;
*ian Fennel Bread Sticks, page 44; Golden Ginger Scones;
l-Pickle Rye Bread, page 44; Coffee-Time Cardamom Braid

Spice and Herb Cookbook 47

Desserts

Streusel Apple Pie

Makes 1 9-inch pie.

- ¾ cup sugar
- 2 tablespoons all-purpose flour
- 1 teaspoon Durkee Apple Pie Spice
- ¼ teaspoon Durkee Grated Lemon Peel
- 6 to 7 cups (about 2 pounds) peeled and sliced tart apples
- 1 9-inch unbaked pie shell
- Streusel Topping (recipe below)

Preheat oven to 375°. Combine sugar, flour, apple pie spice and lemon peel. Lightly toss sliced apples in sugar mixture until well coated. Place in pie shell. Prepare Streusel Topping; sprinkle over apples. Bake 50 minutes. Cover with foil during last 10 minutes to prevent overbrowning.

Streusel Topping

- ½ cup all-purpose flour
- ½ cup chopped nuts
- ⅓ cup packed brown sugar
- 1 teaspoon Durkee Apple Pie Spice
- ¼ cup butter or margarine

Combine flour, nuts, sugar and apple pie spice in bowl; cut in butter until crumbly.

Frost-on-the-Pumpkin Pie

Makes 1 9-inch pie.

- 1½ cups gingersnap cookie crumbs
- ¼ cup butter or margarine, melted
- 1 cup canned pumpkin
- ¼ cup packed brown sugar
- 2 teaspoons Durkee Pumpkin Pie Spice
- 1 quart butter pecan ice cream, softened
- Whipped cream, for garnish

Preheat oven to 350°. Mix together gingersnap crumbs and melted butter; press firmly against bottom and side of 9-inch pie pan. Bake 5 to 7 minutes. Cool. Combine pumpkin, sugar and pumpkin pie spice in small saucepan; cook slowly until heated through; cool. Fold pumpkin mixture into softened ice cream; spoon into crust. Freeze pie 4 to 6 hours or overnight. Garnish with whipped cream.

Old-Fashioned Pfeffernuesse

Makes approximately 4½ dozen.

- ¾ cup molasses
- ½ cup butter or margarine
- 2 eggs, lightly beaten
- ½ teaspoon Durkee Anise Extract
- 4¼ cups all-purpose flour
- ½ cup sugar
- 1¼ teaspoons baking soda
- 1½ teaspoons Durkee Ground Cinnamon
- ¼ teaspoon Durkee Ground Nutmeg
- ¼ teaspoon Durkee Ground Cloves
- ⅛ teaspoon Durkee Ground Black Pepper
- Confectioners' sugar, optional

Combine molasses and butter in saucepan; heat, stirring occasionally, until butter melts; cool. Stir in eggs and extract. Combine flour, sugar, baking soda and spices; gradually add to molasses mixture; mix well. Chill several hours or overnight. Shape dough in 1-inch balls; place on greased cookie sheet. Bake in preheated 375° oven 12 to 15 minutes. Cool. Sprinkle with confectioners' sugar if desired.

Toasty Anise Almond Cookies

Makes 9 dozen.

- 4 eggs
- 1½ cups sugar
- ¾ cup butter or margarine, melted
- 2 teaspoons Durkee Vanilla Extract
- 1 teaspoon Durkee Pure Almond Extract
- ½ teaspoon Durkee Anise Seed, crushed
- 1 cup chopped almonds
- 5 cups all-purpose flour
- 4½ teaspoons baking powder

Preheat oven to 325°. Thoroughly blend eggs and sugar in mixing bowl; stir in melted butter, extracts, anise seed and almonds. Combine flour and baking powder; gradually add to egg mixture; mix thoroughly. Divide dough on floured board into 8 parts; roll each part into a 14-inch rope. Place ropes, 2 inches apart, on greased baking sheet. Bake 20 to 25 minutes until light golden color. Let cool on pan 2 minutes. Increase oven temperature to 375°. Cut each rope diagonally into ¾-inch slices; turn slices onto cut sides. Bake 10 to 15 minutes until lightly toasted. Cool. Store in airtight containers.

Almond Chocolate Spicebox Cookies

Makes 4 dozen.

    1¼ cups all-purpose flour
     1 teaspoon baking powder
    ½ teaspoon powdered instant espresso coffee
    ½ teaspoon Durkee Ground Cinnamon
    ¼ teaspoon Durkee Ground Ginger
    ¼ teaspoon Durkee Ground Cloves
    ¼ teaspoon Durkee Ground Allspice
    ¼ teaspoon Durkee Ground Nutmeg
    ¼ teaspoon salt
    ⅛ teaspoon Durkee Ground Black Pepper
    ⅛ teaspoon Durkee Ground Mustard
    ½ cup butter or margarine
    ⅔ cup sugar
     1 egg
     3 1-ounce squares semisweet chocolate, melted
    ¾ cup slivered almonds

Combine flour, baking powder, coffee and spices; set aside. Cream together butter and sugar in large bowl; beat in egg and chocolate. Gradually add dry ingredients; mix well. Stir in almonds. Shape dough into a roll, 12 inches long and about 2½ inches wide. Wrap in plastic wrap or waxed paper; chill several hours or overnight. Cut dough into slices, ¼ inch thick. Place 1 inch apart on ungreased cookie sheet. Bake in preheated 375° oven 10 to 12 minutes. Remove from cookie sheet and cool on wire rack. Store in airtight containers.

Whole Wheat Cherry Crisps

Makes 4 dozen.

    ½ cup whole bran cereal
    1½ cups whole wheat flour
     1 teaspoon baking powder
     1 teaspoon Durkee Grated Lemon Peel
     1 teaspoon Durkee Ground Cardamom
    ½ teaspoon baking soda
    ½ teaspoon salt
    ½ cup butter or margarine, softened
     1 cup sugar
     1 egg
    ⅓ cup finely chopped Durkee Maraschino Cherries

Preheat oven to 375°. Crush cereal between sheets of waxed paper with a rolling pin; mix with flour, baking powder, lemon peel, cardamom, baking soda and salt; set aside. Cream butter and sugar in a large bowl until light and fluffy; beat in egg and chopped cherries. Stir in flour mixture until smooth. Drop by rounded teaspoonfuls onto ungreased cookie sheets. Bake 8 to 10 minutes or until golden. Cool several minutes on cookie sheets before removing.

Delicate Nutmeg Crisps

Makes approximately 3 dozen.

    ¾ cup butter or margarine, softened
    ¾ cup sugar
    ½ teaspoon salt
    ¼ teaspoon freshly grated Durkee Whole Nutmeg
     3 egg whites
     2 teaspoons Durkee Vanilla Extract
    1¼ cups flour
       Confectioners' sugar, optional
       Durkee Whole Nutmeg, freshly grated, optional
       Cream filling, optional

Blend together butter, sugar, salt and nutmeg until just mixed. Gradually add egg whites and extract; beat well. Add flour and mix well. Cover and chill dough 1 hour. Drop by teaspoonfuls, 2 inches apart, onto greased cookie sheet. Bake 6 to 8 cookies at a time in preheated 375° oven 6 to 8 minutes or until edges are lightly browned. Working quickly, remove each cookie; roll into a thin tube shape. Place on a cooling rack, seam-side down. Shape the next cookie immediately. Cookies will become crisp as they cool. Store in airtight container. Serve sprinkled with confectioners' sugar and freshly grated nutmeg or fill with a cream filling.

Spicy Choc-o-Chip Bars

Makes approximately 8 dozen.

    1½ cups shortening
    1½ cups sugar
    1½ cups packed brown sugar
     4 eggs
     2 teaspoons Durkee Vanilla Extract
     4 cups all-purpose flour
     2 teaspoons baking soda
     2 teaspoons salt
     4 teaspoons Durkee Ground Cinnamon
     1 teaspoon Durkee Ground Cloves
     1 teaspoon Durkee Ground Nutmeg
     1 teaspoon Durkee Ground Coriander
     1 12-ounce package semisweet chocolate pieces

Preheat oven to 375°. Cream shortening and sugars until fluffy. Beat in eggs, one at a time; add vanilla. Combine dry ingredients; blend into creamed mixture. Stir in chocolate pieces. Spread evenly in 2 ungreased 10 x 15 x 1-inch jelly-roll pans. Bake 20 minutes. Cut in 1 x 3-inch bars; cool in pans or on racks.

Variation: Sprinkle chocolate pieces over top of dough before baking. Bake cookies in 3 9 x 13 x 2-inch pans.

Desserts

Gingerbread Spritz

Makes approximately 5 dozen.

1 cup butter *or* margarine, softened
½ cup light molasses
¼ cup packed brown sugar
1 egg
1 teaspoon Durkee Vanilla Extract
2¾ cups all-purpose flour
½ teaspoon baking powder
½ teaspoon Durkee Ground Cinnamon
½ teaspoon Durkee Ground Nutmeg
¼ teaspoon salt
¼ teaspoon Durkee Ground Cloves
¼ teaspoon Durkee Ground Ginger

Cream butter, molasses and brown sugar in large mixing bowl. Add egg and vanilla; beat well. Combine flour and remaining ingredients in small bowl; gradually add to butter mixture; stir until thoroughly combined. Cover and chill 3 to 4 hours. Fill cookie press with half the dough; press into desired shapes onto ungreased cookie sheet. Repeat with remaining dough. Bake in preheated 400° oven 7 to 8 minutes. Allow to cool on cookie sheet 2 minutes; remove to wire rack.

Crackle-Top Molasses Cookies

Makes 4 dozen.

2½ cups all-purpose flour
2 teaspoons baking soda
1½ teaspoons Durkee Ground Mustard
½ teaspoon Durkee Ground Allspice
¼ teaspoon salt
¼ cup shortening
½ cup butter *or* margarine
1 cup packed brown sugar
1 egg
¼ cup molasses
1 teaspoon Durkee Vanilla Extract
1 teaspoon Durkee Imitation Lemon Extract
Granulated sugar

Combine flour, baking soda, mustard, allspice and salt; set aside. Cream together shortening, butter and brown sugar until light and fluffy. Add egg, molasses and extracts; blend well. Gradually add dry ingredients to creamed mixture, stirring until well combined. Cover and chill dough at least 1 hour. Shape into 1-inch balls; dip tops into sugar. Place balls, sugared-side up, about 2 inches apart on greased baking sheet. Bake in preheated 375° oven 10 to 12 minutes or until no imprint remains when cookies are lightly touched. Remove from baking sheet; cool on rack.

Christmas Cutout Cookies or Wreath

Makes approximately 3½ dozen cookies.

¾ cup butter *or* margarine
1½ cups sugar
2 eggs
3 cups flour
1½ teaspoons Durkee Ground Cinnamon
¾ teaspoon Durkee Ground Ginger
1¼ teaspoons baking powder
¾ teaspoon salt
Royal Icing Glaze (recipe below)
Snowcrest Ice-a-Cake and Tips, assorted colors
Snowcrest Write-a-Cake, assorted colors
Snowcrest Decorettes

Cream butter and sugar. Add eggs; beat until fluffy. Set aside. Stir together dry ingredients; add to sugar mixture, blending thoroughly. Chill 1 hour. On lightly floured board, roll out dough to ¼-inch thickness. Cut with floured cookie cutters. Bake on ungreased cookie sheet in preheated 350° oven 10 minutes, or until edges are lightly browned. Cool. Frost with Royal Icing Glaze; decorate with Ice-a-Cake, Write-a-Cake and Decorettes. These make excellent year-round cookies.

Royal Icing Glaze

2 cups confectioners' sugar
¼ teaspoon Durkee Cream of Tartar
2 egg whites

Mix all ingredients in medium mixer bowl on low speed until blended. Increase speed to high; beat 2 minutes. Mixture should be of spreading consistency but not stiff enough to form peaks.

To Make Cookie Wreath: Cut 3-inch wide 14-inch wreath shape from cardboard; cover with foil. Use Ice-a-Cake to adhere cookies to wreath. Position 2 cookies across the width of the wreath, arranging them to overhang edges. Continue positioning until wreath is completely covered. Position a second layer of cookies, placing one cookie atop each cookie pair to achieve a 3-dimensional effect. Decorate with ribbon, if desired.

Top Tier; Gingerbread Spritz; Delicate Nutme Crisps, page 49. Bottom Tier: Cookie Cutout Tray: Spicy Choc-o-Chip Bars (frosted ar unfrosted), page 49; Toasty Anise Almor Cookies, page 48; Old-Fashione Pfeffernuesse, page 4

Desserts

Sesame Coconut Crunch Candy

Makes approximately 1½ pounds.

- 1 cup sugar
- ½ cup light corn syrup
- 1 cup Durkee Sesame Seed
- 1 cup Durkee Flaked Coconut
- 1 teaspoon Durkee Vanilla Extract

Combine sugar and syrup in a 1½-quart casserole. Microwave on High 4 minutes. Stir in sesame seeds. Microwave on High 3 to 5 minutes, until light brown. Add coconut and vanilla, blending well. Microwave on High 1 minute; stir. Pour into shallow buttered 1-quart baking dish. Cut into squares or rectangles with sharp knife while still warm. Cool thoroughly, then wrap each piece separately in plastic wrap.

Chocolate-Covered Candied Ginger

Makes approximately 50 candies.

- ⅓ cup semisweet chocolate pieces
- 1 ounce unsweetened chocolate
- 2 tablespoons butter
- ½ teaspoon Durkee Ground Cardamom or Ground Cinnamon
- 1 2-ounce jar Durkee Crystallized Ginger

Combine chocolate, butter and cardamom in a 2-cup glass measure. Microwave on Medium-Low 2 to 3 minutes until chocolate is melted; stir until thoroughly blended. Remove loose sugar crystals from ginger. Pierce ginger with a toothpick; dip into the chocolate mixture, coating completely. Place on waxed paper; remove toothpick by gently holding ginger with another toothpick. Chill for at least 1 hour.

Gold-Dusted Fudge Balls

Makes approximately 6½ dozen.

- 1 cup (6 ounces) semisweet chocolate pieces
- 1 cup (6 ounces) butterscotch-flavored baking chips
- ¾ cup confectioners' sugar
- ½ cup sour cream
- 2 cups vanilla wafer crumbs
- 1 teaspoon Durkee Grated Orange Peel
- ¼ teaspoon salt
- ¼ teaspoon Durkee Ground Cinnamon
  Durkee Cinnamon Sugar

Melt chocolate and butterscotch chips in a medium saucepan over low heat just until melted, stirring frequently. Mix in sugar, sour cream, crumbs, orange peel, salt and cinnamon. Let stand 30 minutes. Shape into ¾-inch balls; roll balls in cinnamon sugar; chill.

Harvest Pumpkin Fudge

Makes approximately 1¼ pounds.

- 2 cups sugar
- ⅓ cup milk
- ⅓ cup sweetened condensed milk
- ¼ cup canned pumpkin
- 2 tablespoons light corn syrup
- 1½ teaspoons Durkee Pumpkin Pie Spice
- ⅛ teaspoon salt
- 2 tablespoons butter or margarine
- ½ teaspoon Durkee Vanilla Extract

Combine all ingredients except butter and vanilla in saucepan. Cook over medium-high heat, stirring constantly, until mixture comes to a boil. Reduce heat; cook, stirring occasionally, until mixture reaches soft-ball stage (238°). Remove from heat; add butter and vanilla; do not stir. Cool to lukewarm (110°). Beat with a spoon until mixture is very thick, creamy and begins to hold its shape and lose its shine. Pour at once into buttered shallow 1-quart baking dish. Smooth top of fudge; allow to stand until cool and firm. Cut into squares.

Pumpkin Cranberry Torte

Makes 1 8-inch torte.

- 1 18.5-ounce package yellow cake mix (nonpudding type)
- 1 16-ounce can pumpkin
- 2 eggs
- ½ cup water
- 1 tablespoon Durkee Pumpkin Pie Spice
- 1 16-ounce can whole berry cranberry sauce
- 1½ cups Durkee Flaked Coconut
- 1 tablespoon finely chopped Durkee Crystallized Ginger
- 1 teaspoon Durkee Ground Cardamom
- 4 cups whipped cream or nondairy whipped topping, divided
- ½ teaspoon Durkee Pumpkin Pie Spice
  Durkee Crystallized Ginger, optional
  Durkee Flaked Coconut, optional

Preheat oven to 350°. Place cake mix, pumpkin, eggs, water and 1 tablespoon pumpkin pie spice in large mixing bowl; mix on low speed until moistened. Scrape bowl and beaters; beat 2 minutes at medium speed. Pour into 2 greased, waxed paper-lined 8-inch round cake pans. Bake 35 minutes or until done. Cool cakes, then split in half. Combine cranberry sauce, coconut, ginger and cardamom; fold into 2 cups whipped cream. Spread between layers. Fold ½ teaspoon pumpkin pie spice into remaining 2 cups whipped cream; frost cake. Garnish with crystallized ginger and coconut, if desired. Refrigerate.

Zucchini Spice Squares

Makes approximately 20 squares.

    1¾ cups all-purpose flour
    1½ teaspoons baking powder
    ½ teaspoon Durkee Ground Cinnamon
    ½ teaspoon Durkee Ground Cloves
    ½ teaspoon Durkee Ground Nutmeg
    ¾ cup butter or margarine
    ½ cup sugar
    ½ cup packed brown sugar
    2 eggs
    1½ teaspoons Durkee Vanilla Extract
    2 cups (2 to 3 medium) unpared shredded zucchini
    1 cup Durkee Flaked Coconut
    ½ cup chopped walnuts
      Cinnamon Icing (recipe below)

Preheat oven to 350°. Combine flour, baking powder and spices; set aside. Cream butter in a large bowl; beat in sugars. Add eggs and vanilla. Stir in flour mixture until smooth. Stir in zucchini, coconut and walnuts; blend well. Spread in well-greased 9 x 13-inch baking pan. Bake 35 to 40 minutes or until toothpick inserted in center comes out clean. Cool; frost with Cinnamon Icing. Cut into squares.

Cinnamon Icing

    2 cups confectioners' sugar
    3 tablespoons milk
    1½ tablespoons butter or margarine, melted
    2 teaspoons Durkee Ground Cinnamon
    1 teaspoon Durkee Vanilla Extract

Beat all ingredients in a small bowl until smooth.

Coriander Chocolate Pound Cake

Makes 1 10-inch tube cake.

    1 cup butter
    2 cups sugar
    4 eggs
    2¾ cups all-purpose flour
    ½ teaspoon baking powder
    ½ teaspoon baking soda
    ½ cup unsweetened cocoa powder
    2 teaspoons Durkee Ground Coriander
    1 teaspoon Durkee Grated Orange Peel
    ½ teaspoon Durkee Ground Allspice
    1 cup sour cream
    1 teaspoon Durkee Vanilla Extract

Preheat oven to 350°. Cream butter and sugar in a large mixing bowl until light and fluffy. Add eggs, one at a time, beating well after each addition. Combine dry ingredients; add alternately to egg mixture with sour cream, beating after each addition. Stir in vanilla. Pour into a greased 10-inch tube pan. Bake 1 hour and 15 minutes or until done. Cool in pan 10 minutes; turn out on rack.

Maple Apple Cake

Makes 1 10-inch tube cake.

    1 cup dark raisins
    3 cups all-purpose flour
    1 tablespoon baking soda
    1 teaspoon salt
    1 teaspoon Durkee Ground Cinnamon
    ½ teaspoon Durkee Ground Nutmeg
    1½ cups vegetable oil
    1 cup sugar
    1 cup packed brown sugar
    4 eggs
    2 teaspoons Durkee Imitation Maple Flavor
    3 cups (2 to 3 medium) peeled and thickly sliced apples

Cover raisins with water and soak 1 hour; drain. Preheat oven to 350°. Combine flour, baking soda, salt and spices. Beat oil and sugars in mixer bowl until well blended, about 6 minutes. Add eggs, one at a time, beating well after each addition. Add maple flavor and gradually beat in flour mixture; blend well. Fold in apples and drained raisins. Spoon batter into a greased 9-inch tube pan. Bake 1½ hours or until toothpick inserted in center comes out clean. Cool 5 minutes; invert on wire rack.

Old English Seed Cake

Makes 1 10-inch tube cake.

    ¾ cup butter or margarine, softened
    2 cups sugar
    4 eggs
    4 teaspoons Durkee Grated Lemon Peel
    3 cups all-purpose flour
    2½ teaspoons baking powder
    ½ teaspoon Durkee Ground Nutmeg
    ¼ teaspoon Durkee Ground Cloves
    1 cup milk
    1 tablespoon Durkee Caraway Seed
    1 tablespoon Durkee Poppy Seed
    1 tablespoon Durkee Anise Seed

Preheat oven to 350°. Cream butter; add sugar and beat until fluffy. Mix in eggs, one at a time, blending thoroughly; add lemon peel. Combine flour, baking powder, nutmeg and cloves in separate bowl. Add to egg mixture alternately with milk; blend well. Spoon ¼ batter into a lightly greased and floured 10-inch tube pan; sprinkle with caraway seed. Cover with ¼ batter; sprinkle with poppy seed. Top with ¼ batter; sprinkle with anise seed; cover with remaining batter. Bake 1 hour or until a wooden pick inserted in center comes out clean.

Desserts

Apple-Blueberry Crisp

Makes 6 servings.

 3 cups peeled and sliced apples (about 3 apples)
 2 cups blueberries
 ½ cup quick-cooking oats
 ¼ cup all-purpose flour
 ¼ cup packed brown sugar
 ¾ teaspoon Durkee Ground Ginger
 ¾ teaspoon Durkee Ground Cinnamon
 ½ teaspoon Durkee Ground Allspice
 ⅓ cup butter or margarine
   Ice cream, optional

Preheat oven to 375°. Arrange fruit in ungreased 8-inch glass baking dish. Combine oats, flour, sugar and seasonings; cut in butter until crumbly. Sprinkle over fruit. Bake 35 to 40 minutes. Serve with ice cream, if desired.

Vanilla Bean Cheesecake

Makes 8 to 10 servings.

   Butter Crust (recipe below)
 1 3-inch piece Durkee Vanilla Bean
 ½ cup milk
 3 8-ounce packages cream cheese, softened
 1¼ cups sugar
 ¼ cup cornstarch
 4 eggs, separated

Prepare Butter Crust; set aside to cool. Preheat oven to 350°. Split vanilla bean lengthwise; scrape out seeds and pulp. Add pod, seeds and pulp to milk in small saucepan. Heat to simmering; simmer 2 minutes. Remove pod; set aside to cool. Beat cream cheese in large bowl until smooth; gradually beat in sugar and cornstarch until light and fluffy. Beat in egg yolks and cooled vanilla milk. Beat egg whites until stiff peaks form; fold into cream cheese mixture. Pour into prepared crust. Bake 1 to 1¼ hours. Cool on rack. Refrigerate before serving.

Butter Crust

 1 cup all-purpose flour
 2 tablespoons sugar
 ¼ cup butter or margarine
 1 egg yolk, beaten
 2 tablespoons ice water

Preheat oven to 400°. Combine flour and sugar; cut in butter with pastry blender or 2 knives until crumbs are the size of small peas. Stir in egg yolk and water to form a smooth ball. Press onto the bottom of 9-inch springform pan. Bake 8 to 10 minutes or until lightly browned.

Nutmeg Bananas Flambé

Makes 4 servings.

 ½ cup butter
 ½ cup packed brown sugar
 1 teaspoon freshly grated Durkee Whole Nutmeg
 4 firm bananas
 ⅓ cup brandy
 1 quart French vanilla ice cream
   Durkee Whole Nutmeg, freshly grated for garnish

Melt butter and brown sugar in skillet; sprinkle with nutmeg. Cook over medium-high heat, stirring constantly for about 3 minutes or until sauce is golden brown. Slice bananas diagonally in ½-inch-thick slices; add to syrup and heat through, turning gently to coat. Heat brandy in a small saucepan just until warm; ignite and pour, flaming, over bananas. Stir well. Serve over ice cream. Garnish with freshly grated nutmeg.

Tom Thumb Pudding

Makes 8 to 10 servings.

 1 cup snipped, pitted prunes
 1 cup boiling water
 1½ cups all-purpose flour
 1 teaspoon baking soda
 ½ teaspoon baking powder
 ½ teaspoon salt
 ½ teaspoon Durkee Ground Cinnamon
 ¼ teaspoon freshly grated Durkee Whole Nutmeg
 ½ cup sugar
 ½ cup packed brown sugar
 2 tablespoons butter or margarine, melted
   Nutmeg Sauce (recipe below)
   Whipped cream or vanilla ice cream

Preheat oven to 375°. Cover prunes with boiling water; let stand until cool. Stir together flour, baking soda, baking powder, salt and spices in large bowl. Add cooled prune mixture and remaining ingredients, except Nutmeg Sauce and whipped cream; mix well. Pour into ungreased 7 x 11 x 1½-inch baking pan. Top with Nutmeg Sauce. Bake 35 to 40 minutes. Serve warm with whipped cream or vanilla ice cream.

Nutmeg Sauce

 1¼ cups packed brown sugar
 1¼ cups boiling water
 2 tablespoons lemon juice
 1 tablespoon butter or margarine
 1 tablespoon freshly grated Durkee Whole Nutmeg

Combine ingredients, stirring until well blended.

Low Sodium

"Instead of Salt" Seasoning

Makes 3 tablespoons.
Approximately .33 mg. sodium per teaspoon.

2 teaspoons Durkee Garlic Powder
1 teaspoon Durkee Ground Black Pepper
1 teaspoon Durkee Sweet Basil
1 teaspoon Durkee Paprika
1 teaspoon Durkee Onion Powder
½ teaspoon crushed Durkee Sour Salt, optional

Combine all ingredients; mix thoroughly. Store in airtight container. Use as all-purpose seasoning.

Herb Onion Seasoning

Makes ½ cup.
Approximatly .84 mg. sodium per teaspoon.

¼ cup Durkee Instant Minced Onion
1 tablespoon Durkee Sweet Basil
1 tablespoon Durkee Ground Cumin
1 tablespoon Durkee Garlic Powder
1 tablespoon Durkee Cracked Black Pepper

Place all ingredients in blender container; blend on high speed 1 minute or until evenly ground. Store in airtight container. Use as an all-purpose seasoning.

Salt-Free Celery-Herb Blend

Makes approximately 5½ tablespoons.
Approximately 2.63 mg. sodium per teaspoon.

¼ cup Durkee Instant Minced Onion
1 tablespoon Durkee Dill Weed
1 teaspoon Durkee Celery Seed
¼ teaspoon Durkee Tarragon Leaves

Place all ingredients in blender container; blend on high speed 1 minute or until evenly ground. Store in airtight container. Use on vegetables, salads, chicken or seafood.

Salt-Free Savory Herb Seasoning

Makes 2 tablespoons.
Approximately 1.13 mg. sodium per teaspoon.

1 tablespoon Durkee Leaf Marjoram
2 teaspoons Durkee Leaf Thyme
1 teaspoon Durkee Sweet Basil

Place all ingredients in blender container; blend on high speed 1 minute. Or place in small bowl and crush with the back of a spoon. Store in airtight container. Use for seasoning soups, vegetables or pasta.

Zesty Pepper

Makes 5 tablespoons.
Approximately .24 mg. sodium per teaspoon.

2 tablespoons Durkee Ground Black Pepper
1 tablespoon Durkee Paprika
2 teaspoons Durkee Garlic Powder
1 teaspoon Durkee Onion Powder
⅛ teaspoon Durkee Ground Red Pepper

Mix ingredients. Store in airtight container. Use to season meat, poultry or vegetables.

Herbed Salad Dressing

Makes 1½ cups.
Approximately .63 mg. sodium per 2 ounces.

1½ teaspoons Durkee Imported Oregano
½ teaspoon Durkee Sweet Basil
¼ teaspoon Durkee Tarragon Leaves
¼ teaspoon Durkee Garlic Powder
¼ teaspoon Durkee Ground Black Pepper
¼ teaspoon Durkee Onion Powder
¼ teaspoon Durkee Dill Weed
¼ cup water
¼ cup vinegar
1 tablespoon lemon juice
½ teaspoon sugar
1 cup vegetable oil

Place oregano, basil, tarragon, garlic powder, pepper, onion powder and dill weed in blender; blend 15 seconds. Add remaining ingredients; blend 1 minute longer. May be used as a marinade.

Salt-Free Spaghetti Meat Sauce

Makes 1 quart.
Approximately 84 mg. sodium per 1 cup serving.

1 pound ground beef
1 16-ounce can salt-free whole tomatoes with liquid, cut up
1 6-ounce can salt-free tomato paste
1½ cups water
3 tablespoons Durkee Instant Minced Onion
1 teaspoon Durkee Sweet Basil
1 teaspoon Durkee Parsley Flakes
½ teaspoon Durkee Imported Oregano
½ teaspoon Durkee Garlic Powder
½ teaspoon Durkee Ground Thyme
¼ teaspoon Durkee Ground Black Pepper
⅛ teaspoon Durkee Crushed Red Pepper
1 Durkee Bay Leaf

Brown ground beef; drain. Add remaining ingredients. Bring to a boil; reduce heat and simmer, covered, 30 minutes.

Salt-Free Mustard

Makes 1½ cups.
Approximately 2 mg. sodium per tablespoon.

½ cup dry white wine
½ cup water
½ cup white vinegar
½ cup packed brown sugar
5 tablespoons Durkee Ground Mustard
¼ cup Durkee Mustard Seed
1 tablespoon olive oil
2 teaspoons Durkee Onion Powder
1 teaspoon Durkee Garlic Powder
½ teaspoon Durkee Tarragon Leaves
¼ teaspoon Durkee Ground Ginger
⅛ teaspoon Durkee Ground Red Pepper
½ teaspoon Durkee Turmeric

Place all ingredients in blender; blend 1 minute. Pour into top of double boiler; cook, uncovered, over medium heat, until mixture thickens, 30 to 40 minutes, stirring frequently. Pour into sterilized jars; cover and refrigerate.

Hearty Meatball Stew

Makes 6 servings.
Approximately 160 mg. sodium per serving.

Meatballs (recipe below)
1 quart water
3 cups chopped tomatoes (3 large)
1½ cups sliced carrots
¾ cup chopped celery
¼ cup Durkee Instant Minced Onion
1½ tablespoons salt-free chicken bouillon
1 tablespoon Durkee Italian Parsley
⅛ teaspoon Durkee Garlic Powder
1 10-ounce package frozen lima beans

Prepare Meatballs; set aside. Combine all stew ingredients except lima beans in 3- to 4-quart saucepan; bring to a boil. Reduce heat and simmer, covered, 30 minutes. Add lima beans and Meatballs; simmer 15 minutes longer.

Meatballs

1 pound ground pork
⅓ cup dry bread crumbs
1 egg white
½ teaspoon Durkee Italian Parsley
½ teaspoon Durkee Sweet Basil, crumbled
¼ teaspoon Durkee Ground Black Pepper
¼ teaspoon Durkee Fennel Seed, crushed
¼ teaspoon Durkee Imported Oregano, crumbled
⅛ teaspoon Durkee Garlic Powder
1 tablespoon vegetable oil

Combine all ingredients except oil in mixing bowl; mix thoroughly. Form mixture into 1-inch balls. Brown in hot oil in skillet.

Naturally Good Chili

Makes 6 servings.
Approximately 45 mg. sodium per serving.

1 cup dry kidney beans
1 pound ground beef
1 16-ounce can salt-free tomatoes with liquid
3 cups water
3 tablespoons Durkee Paprika
2 tablespoons Durkee Instant Minced Onion
2 teaspoons Durkee Ground Oregano
2 teaspoons Durkee Garlic Powder
1 teaspoon Durkee Ground Cumin
1 teaspoon Durkee Turmeric
½ teaspoon Durkee Ground Black Pepper
½ teaspoon Durkee Crushed Red Pepper
¼ teaspoon Durkee Ground Red Pepper, optional

Soak beans overnight in 1 quart water. Brown meat in a 3- to 4-quart saucepan; drain. Add remaining ingredients including beans and liquid; bring to a boil. Simmer, covered, 3 to 3½ hours until beans are tender. Stir occasionally during cooking.

Salt-Free Herb Bread

Makes 1 loaf.
Approximately 31 mg. sodium per loaf.

1 cup warm water (110 to 115°)
3 tablespoons sugar
1 package active dry yeast
2 tablespoons salt-free butter *or* margarine
1 tablespoon Durkee Parsley Flakes
1½ teaspoons Durkee Sweet Basil, crumbled
½ teaspoon Durkee Imported Oregano, crumbled
½ teaspoon Durkee Leaf Thyme, crumbled
¼ teaspoon Durkee Garlic Powder
2¾ to 3 cups all-purpose flour

Mix water and sugar in large bowl; add yeast and dissolve. Stir in butter, seasonings and about half the flour; mix well. Add remaining flour; stir to a soft dough. Turn out onto a lightly floured board; cover and let stand 5 minutes. Knead dough until smooth and elastic. Place dough in a large lightly greased bowl, cover with a damp cloth, and let rise in a warm place until double in size, 1 to 1½ hours. Punch dough down; turn onto a lightly floured board. Shape into loaf. Place loaf in a greased 5 x 9-inch loaf pan; cover with a damp cloth and let rise until double in size, about 45 minutes. Bake in preheated 400° oven 30 to 35 minutes. Remove from pan; cool on a wire rack.

Pickling and Preserving

Spicy Tomato Catsup

Makes 4 pints.

  13 pounds tomatoes, quartered
  2 cups cider vinegar
  1 cup sugar
  2 tablespoons salt
  2 tablespoons Durkee Liquid Onion
  ½ teaspoon Durkee Ground Red Pepper
  2 teaspoons Durkee Whole Allspice
1½ Durkee Stick Cinnamon, broken
  1 teaspoon Durkee Celery Seed

Fill blender with tomatoes; cover and blend to smooth puree. Pour through strainer or food mill. Process remaining tomatoes in the same manner. Pour tomato puree into large kettle; add vinegar, sugar, salt, liquid onion and red pepper. Tie remaining seasonings in cheesecloth bag; add to puree. Bring to a boil; boil rapidly until volume is reduced by about half. Stir frequently to prevent scorching. Discard spice bag. Pour into hot sterilized pint jars, leaving ½-inch headspace. Adjust caps; process 5 minutes in boiling water bath. Start counting processing time when water returns to a boil. Remove jars; set upright, several inches apart, to cool.

Snappy Dilled Beans

Makes 7 pints.

  4 pounds whole green beans (about 4 quarts)
3½ teaspoons Durkee Mustard Seed
3½ teaspoons Durkee Dill Seed
⅞ teaspoon Durkee Crushed Red Pepper
⅞ teaspoon Durkee Instant Minced Garlic
  5 cups white vinegar
  5 cups water
  ½ cup pickling salt

Wash beans thoroughly; drain and cut into lengths to fill pint jars. Pack beans into hot sterilized jars. Place ½ teaspoon mustard seed, ½ teaspoon dill seed, ⅛ teaspoon crushed red pepper and ⅛ teaspoon minced garlic in each jar. Combine vinegar, water and salt; heat to boiling. Pour boiling liquid over beans, leaving ½-inch headspace. Adjust caps; process 5 minutes in boiling water bath. Start counting processing time when water returns to a boil. Remove jars from water bath; set upright, several inches apart, to cool.

Zesty Italian Sauce

Makes 5 quarts.

  18 pounds fully ripe tomatoes
  3 tablespoons packed brown sugar
1½ tablespoons salt
  ½ teaspoon Durkee Ground Black Pepper
  ½ cup Durkee Instant Minced Onion
  ¼ cup Durkee Parsley Flakes
  1 tablespoon Durkee Sweet Basil, crumbled
  1 tablespoon Durkee Imported Oregano, crumbled
  1 tablespoon Durkee Leaf Thyme, crumbled
  ¼ teaspoon Durkee Ground Bay Leaves
  ¼ teaspoon Durkee Crushed Red Pepper

Remove stem ends, core and chop tomatoes; let stand in colander 15 to 20 minutes to drain. Combine tomatoes, brown sugar, salt and pepper in 10-quart kettle; bring to a boil, stirring occasionally. Reduce heat; simmer, uncovered, 1 hour, stirring occasionally. Puree through food mill; return puree to kettle. Add remaining ingredients; boil gently, uncovered, 1¼ hours or until desired consistency. Pack into sterilized quart jars, leaving ½-inch headspace. Adjust caps; process 55 minutes in boiling water bath. Start counting processing time when water returns to a boil. Remove jars; set upright, several inches apart, to cool.

Salt-Free Dilled Pickles

Makes 2 quarts.

  20 to 24 cucumbers, 3- to 5-inches in length
4½ cups water
  3 cups cider vinegar
  2 tablespoons sugar
  2 tablespoons Durkee Dill Seed
  2 tablespoons Durkee Pickling Spice
  ½ teaspoon Durkee Instant Minced Garlic
  ¼ teaspoon Durkee Powdered Alum
  8 Durkee Peppercorns

Wash cucumbers thoroughly; soak overnight in cold water. Combine water, vinegar, and sugar in 8-quart kettle; bring to a boil. Dry cucumbers; pack into 2 sterilized quart jars. Place in each jar 1 tablespoon dill seed, 1 tablespoon pickling spice, ¼ teaspoon garlic, ⅛ teaspoon alum and 4 peppercorns. Cover with boiling water mixture, leaving ½-inch headspace. Adjust caps; process 20 minutes in boiling water bath. Start counting processing time when water returns to a boil. Remove jars from water bath; set upright, several inches apart, to cool.

Clockwise, from top: Easy Way Dill Pickles, page 60; Homemade Apple Pie Filling, page 61; Freezer Low-Cal Peach Spread, page 61; Corn Relish, page 61; Spiced Blueberry Jam, page 61; Freezer Low-Cal Peach Spread, page 61; Zesty Italian Sauce

Pickling and Preserving

Easy Way Dill Pickles

Makes 9 quarts.

  20 cucumbers, 3 to 4 inches in length
   1 quart water
   1 quart cider vinegar
   3 tablespoons Durkee Pickling Spice,
     tied in cheesecloth bag
  ¾ cup sugar
  ½ cup pickling salt
   9 Durkee Whole Red Peppers (Chillies)
   9 teaspoons Durkee Dill Seed
  2¼ teaspoons Durkee Garlic Powder
  4½ teaspoons Durkee Mustard Seed

Wash, dry and cut cucumbers into halves or quarters lengthwise. Combine water, vinegar, pickling spice bag, sugar and salt in large saucepan; boil gently 15 minutes. Place 1 whole red pepper, 1 teaspoon dill seed, ¼ teaspoon garlic powder and ½ teaspoon mustard seed in each hot sterilized quart jar. Pack pickles in jars; pour in hot liquid, leaving ½-inch headspace. Adjust caps; process 15 minutes in boiling water bath. Start counting processing time when water returns to a boil. Remove jars from water bath; set upright several inches apart to cool.

Crispy Cucumber Slices

Makes 3 to 4 pints.

   2 pounds 3-inch cucumbers (about 25)
   4 small white onions, sliced
   2 green peppers, sliced
  ¼ cup pickling salt
     Ice
   2 cups sugar
  2¼ cups cider vinegar
   1 tablespoon Durkee Mustard Seed
  1½ teaspoons Durkee Celery Seed
  ⅛ teaspoon Durkee Ground Red Pepper

Wash cucumbers; cut crosswise in ¼-inch slices. Layer cucumbers, onion, green pepper, salt and ice in large bowl. Let stand 3 hours in cool place; add more ice if needed. Drain well. Combine sugar, vinegar, mustard seed, celery seed and red pepper in 3-quart saucepan; bring to a boil. Reduce heat to low; add vegetables and simmer until heated through. Stir frequently. Pack vegetables into hot sterilized pint jars; pour hot brine over vegetables, leaving ½-inch headspace. Adjust caps and process 5 minutes in boiling water bath. Start counting processing time when water returns to a boil. Remove jars from water bath; set upright several inches apart to cool.

Lazy Lady Pickles

Makes 5 pints.

   2 quarts (2½ to 3 pounds) thinly-sliced unpeeled
     cucumbers
   1 large red onion, sliced
   1 medium green pepper, sliced
   2 cups cider vinegar
   2 cups sugar
  ¼ cup pickling salt
   1 tablespoon Durkee Mustard Seed
   1 tablespoon Durkee Celery Seed

Combine cucumber, onion and pepper slices in large bowl. Combine remaining ingredients in saucepan; bring to a boil; reduce heat and simmer, uncovered, 5 minutes. Pour over pickles and let stand 30 minutes, stirring occasionally. Place in freezer containers, dividing the juice evenly, and leaving 1-inch headspace; cover. Freeze quickly. Defrost in refrigerator the day before serving.

Purple Plum Mincemeat

Makes 5 pints.

   4 pounds purple plums, unpeeled, quartered and
     pitted
   2 pounds pears, unpeeled, cored and diced
   1 15-ounce box raisins
  1½ pounds light brown sugar (about 3½ cups packed)
  ½ cup orange juice
  ½ cup cider vinegar
  ¼ cup lemon juice
   2 tablespoons Durkee Grated Orange Peel
   2 tablespoons Durkee Ground Cloves
   1 tablespoon Durkee Grated Lemon Peel
   1 tablespoon Durkee Ground Cinnamon
   1 teaspoon salt
   1 teaspoon Durkee Ground Nutmeg
  ½ teaspoon Durkee Ground Allspice

Combine fruits with remaining ingredients in large kettle; bring to a boil. Reduce heat; simmer, covered, 30 minutes. Remove cover; simmer 1 hour until slightly thickened, stirring occasionally. Pour hot mixture into hot sterilized jars leaving ½-inch headspace. Adjust caps; process 20 minutes in boiling water bath. Start counting processing time when water returns to a boil. Remove jars; set upright, several inches apart, to cool.

Corn Relish

Makes 6 pints.

16 ears corn *or* 8 cups whole kernel corn
4 cups chopped cabbage
1 quart white vinegar
1½ cups sugar
1 cup water
1 cup chopped sweet red peppers
1 cup chopped green peppers
1 cup chopped onion
2 tablespoons Durkee Ground Mustard
1 tablespoon salt
1 tablespoon Durkee Celery Seed
1 tablespoon Durkee Mustard Seed
1 tablespoon Durkee Turmeric

Place ears of corn in boiling water; boil 5 minutes; cut corn from cob. Combine all ingredients; simmer 20 minutes. Bring to a boil, stirring constantly; ladle into hot sterilized pint jars, leaving ½-inch headspace. Adjust caps; process 15 minutes in boiling water bath. Start counting processing time when water returns to a boil. Remove jars; set upright, several inches apart, to cool.

Spiced Blueberry Jam

Makes 4 half-pints.

1 pint ripe blueberries, washed and crushed
3 cups sugar
1 tablespoon sliced lemon rind
1 tablespoon lemon juice
¼ teaspoon Durkee Ground Allspice
¼ teaspoon Durkee Mace
3 ounces liquid fruit pectin
Paraffin, melted

Combine berries, sugar, lemon rind, lemon juice and spices in 8- to 10-quart kettle. Bring to a full rolling boil, stirring frequently. Stir in pectin, return to full boil; boil 1 minute. Remove from heat; skim foam off with a metal spoon. Pour into sterilized jars. Seal with ⅛-inch melted paraffin.

Freezer Low-Cal Peach Spread

Makes 4 half-pints.

3 pounds peaches, peeled, pitted and cut up
¼ cup sugar
⅓ cup lemon juice
1 Durkee Stick Cinnamon, broken
1 Durkee Vanilla Bean, cut in pieces
2 Durkee Whole Cardamom Seed, pods cracked
1 tablespoon sugar
1 envelope (¼ ounce) unflavored gelatin

Place peaches, sugar and lemon juice in saucepan; slowly bring to a boil. Tie cinnamon, vanilla and cardamom loosely in cheesecloth bag. Place in peach mixture; boil 2 minutes. Reduce heat; simmer, uncovered, 30 minutes, stirring frequently. Discard spice bag. Blend together sugar and gelatin; sprinkle over hot peach mixture; mix thoroughly. Pour into sterilized half-pint jars leaving ½-inch headspace. Cover containers; cool. Refrigerate or freeze for longer storage.

Spiced Apple Marmalade

Makes 6 half-pints.

6 medium apples, peeled, cored and finely chopped (about 6 cups)
1½ cups water
1 lemon, seeded and thinly sliced
¼ cup orange juice
4 Durkee Stick Cinnamon
½ teaspoon Durkee Whole Cloves
4 Durkee Whole Cardamom Seed, pods cracked
5 cups sugar
Paraffin, melted

Combine apples, water, lemon and orange juice in 8- to 10-quart kettle. Tie spices in cheesecloth bag; add to kettle. Bring to a boil; reduce heat and simmer, uncovered, 10 minutes or until apples are tender. Add sugar; bring mixture to a full rolling boil, stirring constantly. Continue boiling and stirring until thickened and clear (220°), and jelly sheets from metal spoon. Remove from heat; discard spice bag. Skim if necessary. Pour into sterilized jars. Seal with ⅛-inch melted paraffin.

Homemade Apple Pie Filling

Makes 5 quarts *or* enough for 5 9-inch pies.

4½ cups sugar
1 cup cornstarch
1 tablespoon Durkee Apple Pie Spice
¾ teaspoon Durkee Ground Coriander
10 cups water
5½ to 6 pounds tart apples, peeled, cored and sliced
3 tablespoons lemon juice

Blend sugar, cornstarch and spices in large saucepan; stir in water. Cook until thick and bubbly, stirring frequently. Toss apple slices with lemon juice to prevent browning; pack into hot sterilized jars, leaving 1-inch headspace. Ladle hot syrup over apples in jars, leaving ½-inch headspace. Adjust caps; process 20 minutes in boiling water bath. Start counting processing time when water returns to a boil. Remove jars; set upright, several inches apart, to cool.

Spiced Pomander Ball (Nonedible)

Orange, lemon *or* **lime**
Durkee Whole Cloves
Durkee Ground Cinnamon
Orrisroot (can be purchased at pharmacy)
Net
Ribbon

With a skewer point, make holes in a thin-skinned orange about ⅛ inch apart, at random rather than in straight line so skin will not split. Insert cloves in holes to cover entire surface of fruit. Combine equal parts cinnamon and orrisroot; roll clove-studded fruit in cinnamon mixture to completely coat. Store in dry place, on foil-covered tray, 3 to 4 weeks or until fruit shrinks and hardens. Wrap pomander in net; tie with ribbon.

Bouquet Garni

Makes 1 bouquet garni.

1 teaspoon Durkee Parsley Flakes
1 teaspoon Durkee Leaf Thyme
1 teaspoon Durkee Sweet Basil
1 teaspoon Durkee Leaf Marjoram
1 teaspoon Durkee Celery Flakes
½ teaspoon Durkee Leaf Sage
½ teaspoon Durkee Rosemary Leaves
½ teaspoon Durkee Grated Lemon Peel
2 Durkee Bay Leaves

Tie herbs in cheesecloth bag. Use to flavor 2 quarts soup or stew. Seasonings may be adjusted to personal taste.

Spiced Oranges

Makes 4 pints.

8 to 10 oranges
4 cups sugar
1 cup white vinegar
½ cup water
10 Durkee Whole Cloves
2 Durkee Stick Cinnamon
Paraffin, melted

Cut unpeeled oranges into ½-inch slices; remove seeds and discard end pieces. Place oranges in saucepan; cover with water. Bring to a boil; reduce heat and simmer, covered, 1 hour. Drain. Combine remaining ingredients in saucepan; bring to a boil. Cook 5 minutes over medium heat, stirring constantly. Add oranges; simmer, covered, 1 hour. Pack orange slices into hot sterilized pint jars; fill with syrup, leaving ½-inch headspace. Seal with ⅛-inch layer of melted paraffin.

Kahlua

Makes approximately 7 cups.

2½ cups sugar
¼ cup instant coffee
2 cups boiling water
1 fifth vodka (100 proof)
1 Durkee Vanilla Bean

Mix sugar and coffee; add boiling water; stir until sugar and coffee are dissolved. Allow to cool. Stir vodka into cooled mixture; place in wine bottles or fruit jars. Cut vanilla bean in half lengthwise and across; place equal amounts of vanilla bean pieces in the jars of vodka mixture. Close tightly; store in dark place 30 days. Strain and bottle.

Spiced Ornaments (Nonedible)

⅓ cup applesauce
1 tablespoon Durkee Ground Allspice
1 tablespoon Durkee Ground Cinnamon
1 tablespoon Durkee Ground Cloves
1 tablespoon Durkee Ground Ginger
1 tablespoon Durkee Ground Mace
1 tablespoon Durkee Ground Nutmeg
2 teaspoons orrisroot powder (can be purchased at pharmacy)
Durkee Whole Cloves *or* **Whole Allspice**
Toothpicks
Ribbon *or* **string**

Thoroughly combine applesauce, ground spices and orrisroot in small bowl. Form mixture into 1½-inch balls, bells, Christmas trees or other interesting shapes, or roll out mixture to ¼-inch thickness and cut with tiny cookie cutters. If mixture dries while working with it, add a few drops of water. Decorate with whole cloves or whole allspice. Insert toothpicks in top of ornament to make holes for ribbon or string hangers. Leave toothpick in place while drying. Dry*. Remove toothpicks; glue ribbon or string in holes for hangers. Hang near lights on tree for full aroma.

Microwave Oven Drying Instructions: Place ornaments on glass pie plate or paper plate. Microwave on Low 15 to 20 minutes or until thoroughly dry. Turn halfway through cooking time. Ornaments may be slightly soft when first removed from oven. Time varies with microwave and thickness of ornaments.

Conventional Oven Drying Instructions: Preheat oven to 250°; bake 2 to 2½ hours or until dry. Turn halfway through baking time. Time varies with thickness of ornaments.

ockwise, from top: Spiced Oranges; Kahlua;
iced Ornaments; Spiced Pomander Ball

Index